Your Corner
of the
Universe

A GUIDE TO
SELF-THERAPY THROUGH
JOURNAL WRITING

Your Corner of the Universe

ANDREA CAMPBELL

BOB ADAMS, INC.
PUBLISHERS
Holbrook, Massachusetts

Published by Bob Adams, Inc.
260 Center Street
Holbrook, Massachusetts 02343

ISBN: 1-55850-257-2

Printed in the United States of America.

J   I   H   G   F   E   D   C   B   A

This book is available at quantity discounts for bulk purchases. For information, call 1-800-872-5627.

This publication is designed to provide accurate and authoritative information with regard to the subject matter covered. It is sold with the understanding that the publisher is not engaged in rendering legal, accounting, or other professional advice. If legal advice or other expert assistance is required, the services of a competent professional person should be sought.
— From a *Declaration of Principles* jointly adopted by a
Committee of the American Bar Association and a
Committee of Publishers and Associations

COVER DESIGN: Joyce Weston

Acknowledgments

A thank-you to my friend and mentor Alice English, who gives me the periodical jolt of encouragement I need to place myself in the typing chair day after day.

A special thanks to Neil McCluskey, my agent, who discovered me on a computer screen glowing in Florida and plucked me out to sell this project.

Thanks to the colleagues, teachers, and specialists who gave such honest instructional interviews on journal writing. James W. Pennebaker is always informative and an inspiration to psychology students everywhere. My gratitude to Amy Mohon for her insights into the hospital world of therapy and her enthusiasm for my work. Julie Landsman deserves laurels for all her input into the varied lives she touches with her creative writing programs, often going where others fear to tread, into the inner cities to work with teenagers and into the hearts of HIV-positive people, who desperately need all our help and understanding. By the way, thank you, Claudia Jones, for introducing me to your sister and for the loan of an important book. Appreciation goes out to Rita W. McClure for her important views on war, trauma, and other vital topics. Thank you too, Father Anthony Becker, for your counseling information and spiritual encouragement.

A tip of the hat goes to Brandon Toropov, without whose interest this book never would have been.

For
my mother
Anna Mary

Contents

Introduction 11

Chapter 1
Options 13

Chapter 2
Motivation and Direction 29

Chapter 3
Innerscape 41

Chapter 4
Journal Self-Esteem 55

Chapter 5
Calendar 73

Chapter 6
Connections 81

Chapter 7
Insights 89

Chapter 8
Questions and Answers 105

Chapter 9
Conclusions 117

Appendix
Thoughts to Write by 123

Alphabetical List of Exercises 149

Index 151

Bibliography 155

Introduction

Who keeps a journal? It used to be that a diary was on every little girl's "wish list." A diary was a secret place where private nonsense— "Went to school, Wendy sits behind me!"—was spilled out to an imaginary "Dear Diary" confidant, then safely hidden behind lock and key (a lock that could be jimmied with a bobby pin).

We have grown up. The diary has grown up.

Obviously, it is important for writers and journalists to record their daily thoughts. A fiction writer uses his or her notebook for creating characters, noting settings, remembering plots, and devising intricate twists; in other words, as a kind of map or outline for the key storytelling elements.

The journal of the non-fiction writer, on the other hand, represents an organizational tool, a kind of catch-all for detail, nuance, and impression. Later, when the story is ready to be drafted, the journal acts as a safeguard source, helping the writer hone his or her material and supplying precise information for a narrower and more focused slant. And always it stands ready to be consulted— checked and rechecked—for the facts so crucial to accurate reporting.

The journal is also an important instrument in the lives of people we might not normally think of when we talk about journal keeping: people like explorers, pilots, divers, and astronauts, who must keep accurate notes of an expedition, the digest of a flight, or the details of a passage or an encounter. Logs are kept by the greatest and smallest sailing ships in ports worldwide. Diary notations and accounts are recorded by commercial pilots, balloonists, and flight travelers, as well as sports trainers and dance instructors, who use them in neighborhood gyms, schools, and clubs.

The psychiatrist's livelihood is based on keeping journals of a patient's profile and of their sessions; the physician's journal and notations may be her basis for diagnosis. Journals are used by justice officers, courtroom reporters, and the law community, to document evidence, record proceedings, and eventually file judgments.

"Well, fine," you say, "How does this help me? How does this record keeping answer questions about my problems and my concerns?" You want specifics when you're hurting. You want to know how writing lots of words—many seemingly unrelated—can help you to cope and make you feel better. This book offers you a wide array of techniques to work through and heal those areas in your life that are troubling you. As you experiment with unsent letters, imagery, portraits of others, rehearsals with yourself, dialogue, time lines, and many other processes, you will feel a purge of unspent feelings. Armed with such tools you will begin to view your problems not as mysterious, as something solved only by God, but as starting places for growth and learning.

I wanted to make a book that was written in a clear, sometimes anecdotal, easy manner. Something that was not clinical or intimidating. A book you could pick up and open to any chapter and have a clear understanding of its contents. A favorite saying of mine, delivered in a speech by John F. Kennedy, goes like this: "When written in Chinese, the word *crisis* is composed of two characters. One represents danger and the other represents opportunity." *Your Corner of the Universe* represents opportunity. Beginning with the principals and techniques professionals rely on in their daily writing and analyses, it will demonstrate how your journal can become the avenue to a personal and healing experience.

Chapter 1

Options

"The unexamined life is not worth living."
— SOCRATES

The Journal: Taking a Fresh Look

Are you surprised to hear that many people are intimidated by the thought of keeping a journal? Writing has gotten a bad rap, and for many it started back in grade school, with the introduction of cursive writing. The teacher would pace the room waving her pointer authoritatively and peering over the students' shoulders. "That letter has a loop here, Larry (or Sue)," she would admonish, and point her stick at the blackboard, demonstrating perfectly formed letters, letters set neatly within permanent tri-level guidelines, slanting ever-so-correctly at one o'clock. "Remember to cross your t's, children."

It didn't get much better in high school. The writing life, from your adolescent viewpoint, now meant "trucking" yourself to English 101, with its endless preoccupation with grammar and syntax. And didn't we *all* feel choked when it came to those dangling participles, subjective verbs, and dependent clauses?

In college, or later on at business seminars, the professor or speaker would refer to his or her journal work and its role in the creative process until you were led to conclude that journals must be the tools of engineers and poets. A journal was a lofty vehicle reserved for the intelligentsia—or, in the case of the well-suited seminar leader, for people who were trying to sell you something. A journal was certainly *not* something you could see as having any application in your own life, not something that would serve your own real situations and your everyday purposes.

Until now. Your new openness and your desire to solve problems have told you that you can no longer keep your mind on automatic pilot. You are looking for hope and expressing a willingness to seek out new ideas. All this has brought you back full circle— back to the idea of writing and self-discovery, journal writing.

Great Journals of the Past

History has given us a rich literature of diaries and journals. The personal lives preserved in these writings are varied and fascinating. Two great male diarists stand out. The first is a seventeenth-century Englishman named Samuel Pepys (pronounced "PEEPS"). Pepys, a reforming naval administrator and the president of the Royal Society, a weekly meeting of distinguished scientists, kept a detailed record of contemporary affairs. His memoirs are regarded not only as a valuable source for historians and students but as interesting reading for anyone needing to understand the climate and times of English history.

The second writer, George Templeton Strong, did historians a great service by faithfully recording his life and times, forty years' worth of American culture from 1835 to 1875. Strong was a lawyer but had a wide variety of interests, from the arts to politics and theater; he even felt compelled to follow local "fires." He sagaciously documented the ups and downs of the economic climate and how it affected business, his friends, and his associates. He was also a close observer of politics and the effects of the Civil War on daily life.

The historical diary has also been a healing diary. For Anne Frank, a thirteen-year-old Dutch Jewish girl who, with her family, lived in hiding from the Nazis for two years (1942 to 1944), her diary provided an outlet for her fantasies and fears. Anne was a girl about whom it was said that "she knew who she was"—and in her diary we follow her thoughts as she strives to find out. About her ordeal in hiding, she wrote, "I expect you will be interested to hear what it feels like to 'disappear'; well, all I can say is that I don't know myself yet. I don't think I shall ever feel really at home in this house, but that does not mean that I loathe it here, it is more like being on vacation in a very peculiar boardinghouse. Rather a mad idea, perhaps, but that is how it strikes me. The 'Secret Annexe' is an ideal hiding place. . ."

A year before Anne's death in a Nazi concentration camp, she wrote a story about the "fearful Anne": "All around us the war raged, and no one knew whether he would still be alive an hour hence . . . . I was frightened, inside and out . . . Suddenly we were startled by two horrible explosions. As though pricked by needles, we sprang to our feet, all of us at once, and ran out into the hall." She goes on to describe fleeing from the city and the revelation of finding herself running into a meadow, bathed under the stars and the shining moon. She says, "I looked up at the sky, and all at once I realized that I was no longer afraid, no longer felt anything at all, that I was quite calm. How crazy that I did not have a thought about my family and even felt no longing for them. I wanted nothing but quiet, and before long I fell asleep right there in the grass under the open sky."

A very different kind of diarist was the French novelist Aurore Dupin Baroness Dudevant—more commonly known by her pseudonym, George Sand. Sand writes often about looking for her own identity, which is unsurprising when you consider that she wore men's clothing and smoked cigars at a time when such things were decidedly *not* done. She often questioned her drive for completeness in androgynous thinking and behavior. "Then a bizarre explanation occurred to me. I was double. There was about me another *I* that I could not see, but which always saw *me*, because it always replied to me. . . .I concluded that all things, all beings, had their reflection, their double, their other I, and I wanted passionately to see mine." Noel Gerson, author of *George Sand—A Biography of the First Modern, Liberated Woman*, thinks that Aurore lived "a century and a half before her time."

The journals of Henry David Thoreau, written between 1837 and 1861, were published after his death in fourteen volumes. In them this great American thinker and writer learned and honed the craft of writing and developed the ideas that were to put their permanent stamp upon American thought and culture. As Thoreau wrote in 1841, "My Journal is that of me which would spill over and run to waste, gleanings from the field which in action I reap, I must not live for it, but in it for the gods. They are my correspondent, to whom daily I send off this sheet postpaid."

President Truman kept diaries. In *Harry S Truman in His Own Words*, author William Hillman remarks, "The President keeps his diaries in black leather notebooks. But his memoranda are written on blocks of paper, five by eight, and none of them have been type-copied or designed in any way for any eyes but his. The President told me that the writing of these memoranda helps him to clarify his thinking and serve as notes for further study and decision. For the first year of his Presidency, Mr. Truman penciled brief but pungent comments on the margin of his daily appointment sheet. For example, after listening to one visitor for fifteen minutes, the President simply wrote: 'Baloney peddler.'"

The diaries of photographer Margaret Bourke-White, whose work includes the cover photo for the inaugural issue of *Life* Magazine, follow her brilliant career, volatile marriage, and illness and eventual demise from Parkinson's disease. She also felt compelled to destroy much about her life history and secrets. Vicki Goldberg, in her book, *Margaret Bourke-White: A Biography*, notes, "As she burned her diaries before she died, certain details were meant to go to the grave with her and undoubtedly many did. Yet perhaps de-spite herself, Bourke-White left behind an intensely personal record of her journey to success, of the unconventional, liberated life she in-vented for herself as a woman on men's territory, and of her attempt to fulfill both her professional ambitions and her domestic yearnings."

Virginia Woolf relied heavily on her diary, so much so that, for example, one can almost see her life slipping away in her entries about the impact of the second World War on her sensibilities. With the advance of each horror, real or imagined, her death by drown-ing, accidental or intended, seems to draw closer. Woolf writes, "All the walls, the protecting and reflecting walls, wear so terribly thin in this war. There's no standard to write for: no public to echo back; even the 'tradition' has become transparent." And closer to her death, "Yes, I was thinking: we live without a future. That's what's queer: with our noses pressed to a closed door. . . ."

In the 12,000-odd diaries that have been published in English you will find history and, most of all, experience. Men's and women's struggles with war, sexual preferences and ideals, thoughts about early feminism, philosophical thinking, world travels, illness, depression and creativity—all have been captured and preserved in their own enduring historical records. These journal-keepers did not start out with the intention of sharing their words and observations in publication. They were simply disciplined and meticulous writers who found in this medium an outlet for their experiences and their emotions. These men and women, common and uncommon, have shown us the value of moments, thoughts, feelings, insights noted down on paper as a lasting record of the process of growth and change.

Why Keep A Journal?

People have all kinds of reasons for starting a journal, as the historical excerpts show. What are yours? Do you want to satisfy a creative urge, to release pent-up emotions? Is this a way to work out self-correction or to clear the air with confession? Will you use your journal to clarify your own unique perceptions or to help you make decisions? Will it be an organizational tool for goal setting, or a way to tap into and resolve questions about the past? Will this be your private domain, a place to retreat to, after a day of nurturing and caring for others, enhanced perhaps by pillows, muted lighting, and hot chocolate? A private niche just for you—yours alone?

Perhaps you want to use your journal as an instrument for tuning in to your own body's rhythms or for providing a balance between peace and risk. You can also make it the place where you celebrate time and events in a more lasting and permanent manner.

There are journal techniques that can help you achieve all these varied goals and more. They take effort, of course, and concentration, and yet that act of creating, patiently and with perseverance, will ultimately carry you along as you feel the results of your own mind's efforts. And results can come in many forms.

Are you hoping to refocus your energies by using them to confront and solve problems, instead of wasting time and emotions feeling tired and depressed after a hard day of putting yourself down? Results for you could mean giving up seeking the support and approval of others and doing instead what you know you would like to be doing. You want to create a feeling of confidence and courage within yourself, an assurance that arrives, as if by silent messenger, after you learn who you are, what you want, and what you can bring to life's table.

Maybe you are seeking relief from the pressures of not having control. Strange things are happening today; we all struggle to make sense of the changes. In this fast-paced world of bits, bytes, and short attention spans, it becomes increasingly difficult to distinguish what is relevant to your own life, your family, and the future.

Life today offers more choices, and demands more decisions. It's tiring making choices, and we often revert to the regular, the usual, the mundane—"I'll have the same." And yet, living amidst so many alternatives has a positive side, too. It can give us a wider spectrum of ideas, stretching us to accommodate new people and sudden changes. As we gain exposure to more and more variables, to the shadings, as it were, between black and white, our tolerance for others expands accordingly. Journal writing can help clarify and facilitate this process.

School did not prepare us for some of the practical lessons we have needed in our lifetimes: Developing loving and lasting relationships, self-knowledge and acceptance, and personal growth; making good use of time; facing the realities of death and the legacy we leave behind. One day we turn around and time seems to be flowing away. Like ingredients folded into a cake, our days blend together in such a way that we cannot distinguish one day from another, we cannot separate the egg from the oil. If we try to remember what has gone by for us, entire months are relegated to a single day's recollection, a significant or special event.

Keeping a journal is one important way to counter this phenomenon. The word *diary* is derived from the Latin *dies*, a day, and the conscious and deliberate act of writing a journal entry can serve to define each day as you work through and examine your feelings, wants, and direction. Such a habit of introspection helps to sort out the blur of years. Collecting and rereading your thoughts, you begin to see a canvas painted with bold, definite strokes of decision, satisfying lines of pattern and direction, and filled-out spaces of events and achievements.

Without life's trials and the struggles of overcoming them, we would never exercise the will to grow, change and become stronger.

Adversity is the impetus for change. Adversity is the banquet, change is the hungry guest, and the food is often bitter. We can let change represent a new determination, or a new defeat. Journal writing will help you to recognize and take pleasure in the adventure—the moments of happiness as well as of struggle. As both a catalyst and a record of growth, it will come to reflect an essential part of who you are, and who you are becoming.

The Book

A journal can take on as many physical appearances and dimensions as there are creative ideas. The parameters are endless.

- ❖ A consultant roughs out proposal plans and ideas and forms questions on a napkin at lunch. Although as a permanent record the napkin leaves something to be desired, this system could nevertheless be called a form of journalism.

- ❖ Someone who spends a great deal of time commuting back and forth to work might find that a micro-cassette recorder best suits his purposes.

- ❖ An extremely visual person or a student of art might want to incorporate her sketches, doodles, or photographs along with her daily musings.

- ❖ People who record their dreams, save clippings from newspapers, or collect quotes, might also be keeping and adding to their personal journals.

Journal books can be as expensive and fashionable as a crocodile-embossed Filofax or as simple as a spiral-bound steno pad. Both could have divider sections filled with facts, practical information, and goals.

- ❖ A student writing in a three-ring binder might feel the need to log the results of tests, create study checklists, and scribble out other areas of interest; to keep track of lecture series and capture conversations with people who have an important effect on his life. He might then decide to save those records and bind them together in a more permanent way for safekeeping.

❖ A researcher or someone who organizes information might feel comfortable filing her daily work—exercises, facts, and quotes, along with her own perceptions—on 4" x 6" lined cards, and storing them in boxes according to date and month.

❖ A performance artist may sketch stories, delineate creative moments, and rehearse future routines in leather-bound volumes small enough to carry around.

❖ A family can write out their concerns and worries, milestone occasions, family trips, and plans for their future growth together in scrapbooks and large cloth-bound books.

❖ Charts and checklists, facts and intuitions can be graphed, charted, and logged into computer databases and spreadsheets, or copied on to disks.

All of these physical dimensions and styles can represent the art of journal writing.

If your goal is to seek uninhibited expression, to kick creativity into high gear, avoid a very small or portable journal. It tends to confine one's entries. Likewise, any book with a rigid date system may make you feel as if a summary of the day is required, or worse yet, that a missed or skipped day is somehow reason for self-reprimand. Tristine Rainer, journal writer and author of *The New Diary*, tells the story of a friend of hers who, when faced with having to write in a calendar book at the age of nine, answered the problem by writing the whole week in advance. He carefully copied "Went to school," "Went to school" at the top of each page, repeating the day's mundane activities.

Experienced journal writers do say that dating your entries is very important for the purposes of reference. It allows the writer to follow growth patterns and aids rereading. It also places the entries in a time context, enabling the writer to keep track of what's current. Should you feel moved to characterize your feelings about world politics or the most recent fads or trends, your observations will set the background for your life at that time and help to explain your thought processes during that era.

If the book you choose is too beautiful or intimidating, if it seems too perfect to spoil with clumsy words, take steps to make certain that the next volume you buy allows you to feel unencumbered. Personal adjustments as to the size, shape, and overall feel will determine whether your book fulfills its task of inspiring, making you feel artsy, or providing a comfortable setting for the work of self-discovery and setting goals.

You might want to make a list of the qualities you prefer and then hunt for what suits you by checking out bookstores, office-supply houses, gift shops, and stationery stores. The first questions you will ask are, What size and shape is best? Do I care about the color and cover design? Will I be carrying it around, and if so, will it be sturdy enough to withstand trips? Do I want to be able to bind loose pages when a volume or time period is complete, or would I feel better starting off with something bound? (If it happens that scraps of paper are the only thing available to you at a particular time of inspiration, keep a master volume that you can later tape or paste the papers into.)

Would I feel more confident with lined pages, or do I want to be able to scribble, draw, cluster, and have a free hand on any page? You name it, it's out there: blank books, lined books, books with sayings printed in them, women's journals and scrapbooks, spiral-bound books, ring binders, legal pads . . .

Consider your writing implement, too. Pencil allows you to erase, of course, but it is not very permanent and it often comes out too light. It may also erode with time, and if you ever give in to the temptation to go back and erase later, you will almost certainly regret it. Christina Baldwin, a popular leader of journal workshops for women, says she prefers the unrestrained flow and feel of ink oozing onto paper from a fountain pen.

Whatever you choose, choose something that makes you feel like the journal writer who, when she touched the well-worn, personally designed cover of her book, felt "a sense of comfort, security, and well-being like an old familiar pillow that remembered, and molded to, the shape of my head."

You might think it a good idea to create a series of books, one for recording dreams, another for setting goals, and still another for regular writing. But this serializing has a tendency to stifle what may be coming fast by framing it small or giving it artificial borders. The temptation might be to stop the flow and reserve the feeling in order to record it in another volume. (Where did the feeling go?) How much easier to integrate it all in one volume, where you can observe your progression from emotional thinking to programmatic planning to chasing fantasies and dreams, in recurring patterns.

Once you have decided what kind of book is best for you, the next consideration is what time of day to write. You may have decided to keep your journal next to your bedstand and recap the day's events. All day long you have thought about your feelings and you are eager to write them down. But almost from the moment you actually snuggle down to write, your energy wanes. Fatigue sets in and your mind is a mush, clumsy and slow. You long to rest, not write.

For some, the answer to this dilemma may be no more complicated than choosing to begin writing first thing in the morning when they are rested. Last night's dreams are surely remembered best *before* you have had time to let them dissipate with conversation or to dissolve like the sugar in your morning coffee.

If your days are exceptionally full of stress or complicated with roller-coaster emotions, entries both morning and night may provide you with a release from the day's tensions. You can write out your feelings at night, and in the morning, with its change of pace and more tranquil outlook, devote yourself to introspection. At that time of day you may be more clear-headed, not to mention better rested. At any rate, you are going to want to express yourself and look for answers when you are in a variety of moods—the weird, illogical, extreme, and absurd moments of your life as well as the smooth transitional times.

Let the returning to your writing become a ritual, something associated with getting ready for bed or readying yourself for a new day. Maybe you will set aside pleasurable writing time along with your regular phone calls or correspondence, or after reading the daily newspaper. If you are worried about misplacing your book if you take it out of the house, take along pieces of paper and paste or tape them into your journal later, keeping an uninterrupted flow.

Above all, keep what you write strictly to yourself. With the aid of your journal, you will often be taking a good, honest look at yourself, which is not the easiest thing to do. Realize that you will make mistakes and that, at times, it will be embarrassing, even scary, to admit your faults and dreams in writing. You will be embarking on a discovery of what contributed to making you who you are. You will want to record what thrills, infuriates, excites, shocks, and disturbs you. Your goal will be to write uncensored material.

For certain effects you may feel that you need to pretend, create fantasies, or follow hunches. The truth, or what you then believe to be the truth, will be in a state of evolution or just emerging. Sometimes the truth is less the real facts of the situation and more a continuous revelation. In other words, the things you believe on the first go-around may later, with self-questioning, be the very things you finally reject.

Perhaps your material stands to hurt someone else or be misunderstood by others. Perhaps you do not want the vulnerability of exposing your personal secrets to others. These are all valid reasons for keeping your journal private.

Often, to be able to work through our moods, we need *not to repress* the desire to be negative but to release it. On a simpler level, we may just feel the need to be able to write sloppily and ungrammatically, to use profane language and shocking images. How wonderful it is to have the freedom to express yourself without having to explain or be judged by others.

Take a moment, too, to look at journal writing from the perspective of observers. If you happen to be in the midst of a troubled or unhealthy relationship, might not the other person look at your private writings as a threat? Your moments apart or your request for undisturbed time might be interpreted as a vehicle for revenge, a weapon you use to articulate your grievances. If your lover is feeling uncertain about the partnership, your new journal activity may appear to represent an assertion of independence. Perhaps it demonstrates a sense of individuality that the other person still lacks. He or she may then interpret your need for privacy as a rejection. Stand firm. Whatever the pressure, do not allow your journal to be opened for inspection. Better to resolve your insecure relationships by communicating directly and openly than feel obligated to offer your writings up to the scrutiny of another.

If you do feel a need to expose your writing, ask yourself what you hope to gain by sharing your journal with someone else. Are you hoping the difficult person will be transformed by your new-found beliefs and changes? What results are you looking for? And are you ready for complications, misunderstandings, and unforseen consequences—such as the person's becoming jealous of your profound inner life? Why not instead take this opportunity to institute new pattern of mutual respect and trust within the family by announcing in a firm but friendly manner, "These are my private times and I need to be left alone so that I can concentrate." Tension over possessions, territory, and time for self is often best resolved before conflicts arise by talking, finding amicable direction, and setting similar goals in a verbal pact.

A good way to indicate to your family that you need to carve out time for reflection and writing is simply to remind them of their own need for private time. They sometimes want to be alone to read, practice music, or play computer games. Plant the seed that you would like some quality relaxation time for yourself—then take it.

One way to keep your private book private is to store it with your other personal affects. Leaving it sitting out with other papers, magazines, or general reading—in the stream of traffic—only encourages curious family members to take a peek. The temptation is too great. There sits a private book, your *I-me-mine* place, the mere sight of which screams, "This ought to be interesting." The very word "journal," indeed, conjures up thoughts of private creative genius and provocative secrets.

Forget about writing in code or some pre-conceived short-hand. You'll soon tire of espionage, and rereading it will quickly become a chore.

One woman concerned with her journal's privacy found that the best place to keep it was with her cookbooks. She was certain no one would ever look there. Maybe you should consider storing yours with the car waxing supplies or the dog shampoo.

Format
The two most reassuring things to remember about journal writing are that everything you need to know is inside you, and that everyone's brain, as a creative, interpretive device, enjoys filling in details and solving problems.

Of course, though we use words like "writer" and your "writing," this does not imply that your journal should imitate books. As Judith Moore says in her article entitled, "Save Your Life: Notes on the Value of Keeping a Diary," "A perpetual work-in-progress, the diary has no structure, no plot, no theme. Most often, it is written in an eternal present tense, a privileged position between past and future."

Another consideration before you begin is to let yourself enter into a positive but not necessarily "correct" attitude. It may help, as you embark on this new-found process, to think of it as a sort of creative adventure, not a trial. Anaïs Nin, who has published six volumes of her diary along with critical studies and countless essays and novels, says in one of her entries, "I have just opened a new notebook and made a new friend. I have just closed a notebook which is already full, and here I am with blank pages to fill, and I hope with all my heart to be able to write things in it that I shall never be ashamed of. After a few days, dear new notebook, you will know me very well and will become acquainted with my ideas and the meanderings of my mad imagination."

Nin adds a note to herself about continuing—that she will try to write faithfully and sincerely every day—and she says she will write in her books with the same pen and file them under the same name as her other works. She regards her journal writing as a discipline, and for many that is just what it is. If you are undertaking a journal for the first time, give it a fair amount of time, a good several months, to take hold. Avoid making conscious judgments too early, or you may be setting yourself up for failure and disappointment. Honestly, writing should express the spectrum of living, which some days, is mundane and ordinary and other days just the opposite. On the one hand, you might want to head toward your journal whenever you are feeling off-balance, keeping in mind that every life cycle has its highs and lows. At times it may seem as if you are continually coming upon new questions instead of answers to the old. But by taking this first promising initiative to bring your unconscious thoughts into a conscious format, you are on the way to exposing unrealistic expectations, discovering what really is, finding out what shapes you, taking that knowledge and converting it into what can be, and then letting go of the rest.

On the other hand, it's not unusual to live through periods of being, well, boring. There is a lot of sameness in the world, and its presence often serves to offset conflict, so don't fear boringness or try to deny it. Truth is often the sum of all kinds of different thoughts and feelings.

If you ever get a chance to read published or historical diaries, you will notice that they are often not the most gripping reading, Yet taken in context, they can prove illuminating in a more philosophical way. Imagine, when you sit down to write, that you are casting your line into a sea of deeply felt emotions, and realize that people in transitions often lose their catch again and again. Anticipate, furthermore, that a mind-shift to meaningful self-discovery will take time.

One fascinating phenomenon that will quickly take hold of you as you get into the habit of writing—though you may declare with certainty that it will never happen to you—is what I call "experiencing your critic."

Since much of self-expression is unknown territory, our minds are often filled with contradictions, and we try to do what we think is right. This will assert itself in our striving for perfection, the urge to correct grammar, erase, or, when really critical, to cross words out. Try to tell your mind to curb these tendencies. You'll still make judgments about what you've written, or worry that a comment that suddenly shows up is "not nice." *Did I really say that?* Leave it lie; it needs to be said. It came from the subconscious and cut in front of the line for quick service.

We come to this writing with a lot of excess baggage. All of us have preconceived and family-shaped notions about what we think is correct, just, or morally right. Our leftover feelings of guilt are often self-imposed, and it will be very difficult at times to let our hand write the truth. Start head-on with the premise that nothing is out of bounds. There are no game rules. You can scream, brag, curse, lie, and misspell words. It's perfectly okay to paste things in, to write sideways or upside-down. Complaining is encouraged. There are no roles to play; no subject is taboo. Write in a new language, change your point of view, list the ugly opposite the beautiful. Exaggerate. Try your hand at poetry. Be corny. Let yourself go!

If this is still not freeing enough, think of writing as you talk out loud or pretend you are in conversation. This will create your style, your voice. Write fast and let it flow so that you will not censor, condemn, or be stifled.

Perfection is for mannequins, not for real people with unkempt hair and chipped fingernails.

Creative Action Checklist

- ❖ Avoid the small, needling frustrations in daily life by making copies of car keys and buying extra batteries, scissors, and other things you use a lot of.

- ❖ Push back the furniture, roll up the carpet, turn up your most inspiring, beat-driven music, and dance.

- ❖ Paste occasional new articles, news of current fads or trends, and photo clippings or quotes into your journal for historic reference.

- ❖ Invest time into things done for aesthetic reasons only: meditate with headphones on and feet propped up; rent a comedy video; give things away; read a biography.

- ❖ Create time between frenetic activities by, for instance, mapping out your day before getting into your car for work and walking around the block before entering the house at the end of the day. After paying bills, take a hot bath and bring your journal, then force yourself to stay in until the hot water gets cold.

Creative Comfort Checklist

- ❖ For older readers, recall your life at twenty. How has your life improved? What passions or concerns would you like to respark or take on? What skills have you mastered, or forgotten about?

- ❖ Write down the definitions and the differences between the words "stress" and "busyness."

- ❖ Make a list of 40 things you love.

- ❖ Do things differently. Use your opposite, not your dominant hand to comb your hair, turn doorknobs, etc.

- ❖ Women: Buy a new pillow—attach a potpourri sachet to it. Men: Buy a new footstool or slippers.

Chapter 2

Motivation and Direction

"A well-written life is almost as rare as a well-
spent one."
— THOMAS CARLYLE, *Richter*

Neurologist Richard Restak observes that dealing with the daily raw
emotions of patients has made many doctors involved in similar
professions choose paths of self-destruction. In his book *The Brain
Has a Mind of Its Own*, he claims that writing things down has helped
him to make order out of life's chaos, and that switching between
his two very different career activities, physician and author, gives
his life stability.

The balance for him, then, is between the frenetic activity and
turmoil of the clinic, on the one hand, and the slow-blossoming
ideas of writing and what he calls "productive passivity" on the
other. Restak also suggests that he has come to know the different
energies needed to juggle these very different professions and says
he does not push writing until the hyperactivity that comes with his
clinical work leaves him.

Restak has found what works for him. You will also find what
works for you, a voice and a rhythm to express your thoughts within
the confines of your personal territory and private mind.

The patterns and motivations suggested here may appear to
some as gimmicks, diversions, or antics. So be it. Try them on as if
you were a beginning artist learning a new free-flowing dance step.

If you find you are consciously stepping on your own toes, experiencing an off-balance sensation, or feeling tense after practicing a particular method for a while, try a different approach. This is your own production, and there are many different moves to choose, sample, learn, or discard.

At times you will experience great frustration and a conscious resistance against trying anything that seems to produce no results. Try not to visualize the journal as a finished product but more like a continuing process, following a recipe, like learning to play the piano, or charting a trip. If, in the process, you change an attitude or modify your behavior, you have succeeded in rearranging a lifetime of learned pattern, and some would call that a miracle.

In creating a map for this writing journey, you will probably find it easier to keep the writing devices and techniques presented here distinct. Try one method for a week or so, then check out something new. Bear in mind that various methods will seem to overlap and may sometimes produce surprisingly similar outcomes. Perhaps this is your unconscious waving a flag and asking you to address a problem, or it could be a thought begging for recognition or a feeling just beginning to germinate.

For simplicity's sake, the techniques are divided up into four categories: Seeking and Examining; Tapping the Creative Unconscious; Venting, Realizing, and Coping; and Planning Goals. Within each of these sections, different writing samples or exercises are described, some of which will suggest their own best applications. For example, if you are having trouble with a relationship, you may want to first look under the Seeking and Examining category and try the exercise called "Sketches of Others."

If, on the other hand, you are writing for your own sense of discovery and you feel intimidated by specifics, you may wish to begin by writing about your feelings. You could describe your most recent incident of great emotional intensity and see whether this gets your creativity flowing.

For a sense of direction, that is, a sense of how to address the writing, think of yourself as the someone you will be in a month or in a year, and ask, what would you like the future You to know or remember? You may feel a need to describe what your life has been like or is like since you got married, moved to a new area, or were hospitalized. Indicate the main characteristics of what's important to you in the present; don't worry about missing details. As Dr. Restak, the neurologist cited earlier, points out, "The brain never forgets anything it has once learned—even though we may not be capable of putting that knowledge into words or even consciously recalling it."

The important thing is to let the writing happen. Don't deny an urge or worry about what's wrong. If the milestones in your life are not the impetus for your free-flow writing, begin with pushing beyond the boundaries of the current day. Look at a photograph, or close your eyes and imagine flying overhead, looking downward at a meaningful period in your life.

In *A Natural History of the Senses*, writer Diane Ackerman outlines techniques used by writers to invite their inspiration. Ackerman tells us that the poet Schiller used to keep rotten apples under the lid of his desk and inhale their pungent bouquet whenever he needed to find the right word. Even after Schiller closed the drawer to begin his writing, the heady fragrance remained in his memory. Yale University researchers have also discovered, says Ackerman, that a spiced apple's piquant smell has a powerful elevating effect on people and can avert panic attacks. Apparently, Schiller's strange habit seems to have been grounded in common sense.

The techniques and devices presented here are just that, tools to enable you to open up to writing and to make you feel comfortable enough to use your reserves and capabilities to discover more about your life, its purpose, and the possibilities for life's fulfillment.

Seeking and Examining

Centering

Centering is personal homework. By this means you approach your thinking from one person's point of view, the "I" structure. The ultimate goal here is to coax out the voice of your mind and body.

As grown-ups we are the products of our parent's influence, our education, and our experience. With centering you try to determine the difference between what was and how *you perceived it*. As our lives become more complicated and rushed, we often resort to what comes easy at the expense of what we really want. So centering is finding out what we really believe and want.

Don't think of yourself as a reporter who records weather statistics, tells the latest poll results, or outlines the best traffic patterns. Ignore the tendency to write accounts: "It was a rainy, wet day." Instead, try to express what feeling compelled you to watch the water droplets racing down the window pane, how you perceived their influence on you, and what insights you gained from that experience.

Your perceptions may be about people, heroes, or characteristics you admire in other people; the effect of nature on your well-being; or how looking at modern art makes you feel—not about what books you've read or are reading. But if a book does persuade you to feel a different way, and if you have changed your thinking about a subject after reading it—that's a source for journal material.

Vivid details, the observation of the minute and the obscure, may help you to get a handle on this kind of writing. For example, you might write about how you perceived your parents in a difficult situation when you were a child under their care. If your father grew impatient and yelled at your mother when the car got a flat tire on a family trip, how did you perceive that behavior? Did it influence the way you look at similar problems today? Does your tendency for optimism come from your mother's effect on your personality? Did she explain the booming thunder during violent storms by saying, "God is bowling in heaven"? Again, how do such childhood interactions influence your feelings today?

If you find yourself writing with humor, you have probably come to a conclusion about the subject already and are dealing with it in your own best manner. Being able to view something's effect on you lightheartedly suggests that you have already distanced yourself from your painful thoughts, and this is your way of coping. Note what it is exactly that your humor has brought forward and learn from that. "I can laugh at _____ now because. . . ."

Word Portraits

Word portraits are a process of clarifying what your position is in relationship to another person. They serve two major causes: helping you both to see others as separate individuals, rather than focusing on what you need from them, and to explore the relationship in such a way as to reveal as much about the writer as the person being described.

For example, if you were to write a word portrait of your child, your mate, or a friend, you might describe the person as manipulative, aloof, or some other descriptive term that sheds light on that person's particular impact on your psyche. In this way, if your observations are objective, you remove your relationship from the context of what you want from the person—honesty, conversation, etc.—and substitute the realization that he or she exists as a unique individual with characteristics that set him or her apart from you. As an end result, you may find yourself able to change your approach to your relationship with that person.

Once you have sketched your person with words, ask yourself questions. What fascinates or attracts you to this person? List his or her endearing qualities, then list the negative ones, or those that bring out negative feelings in you. Have you highlighted qualities you would like to develop in yourself? Or are your observations really serving to point out what you need to improve in *your own* nature?

Word portraits can, of course, be used to help illuminate the easy assumptions of our friendships, such as expecting someone to be your guru, potential lover, or best friend in times of transition or need. Failure to face these unspoken expectations squarely will set you up for feelings of disappointment and abandonment again and again. Since there are no guarantees or contractual arrangements with friends, making a chart of your expectations and what you think theirs are can lead you to new levels of sharing and freedom.

This process can also be applied to your business relationships. What can you learn by looking at your boss, colleagues, and subordinates? More importantly, what characteristics do they bring out in you? Much of the stress of business relationships arises from poor communication and false expectations. Word portraits, like clues in a mystery novel, should help bring about better understandings.

Lists

Lists are one of the most popular self-help tools, with good reason. They are simple, informative, and to the point. If we are in a hurry, or need to compress a large amount of history into a manageable size, lists can help. Use the milestones of your life—birth, moving, marriage, the dates of growing up—as your sign posts.

Lists may also be used to record your feelings and to outline your impressions of people and events. At the start of a popular children's novel by Lois Lowry, ten-year-old Anastasia Krupnick makes two lists. All the things she loves are on the left side, and all the things she hates are on the right. As Anastasia grows in understanding, the lists are periodically updated, and the reader notices that the character of the little girl is beginning to evolve. At the end of the book, Anastasia's hate list is entirely crossed out and every item moved over into the love column. Something like this can happen in real life as well as in the world of fiction. Consciously and unconsciously, through the help of lists, you can track your own growth and understanding.

Lists can include: the best and worst things; current beliefs or commitments; expectations; success goals and business steps; a personal chronology, starting with birth, first pain, first date, important calendar "firsts," and so on, up to the current day.

You might want to consider making a list of what "security" means to you. What comes after food and shelter; what exactly is it that makes you feel safe? Do you feel secure in your health and accept your physical self? Is there a trust and security in your friendships? Are you comfortable knowing you have emotional independence, and do you have your own set of values over and above those of your parents? Economic independence is often an integral part of a man's sense of security, the knowledge that he has the resources to take care of his needs and those of his family. The security list will quickly point up your strengths, your shortcomings, and the areas where you are most vulnerable, and it will give you an idea of what areas to target when you decide you can take on new risks and live more creatively.

Benjamin Franklin made a list of the thirteen virtues he was seeking, including frugality, tranquility, and humility. Franklin even went so far as to chart his progress on a graph. For some this could quickly become an exercise in nagging, and in this case a more positive approach to lists would be preferable.

Fact Check

Unappealing as it may sound, a fact check is a device to keep you honest, to keep you from fooling yourself. What you are trying to achieve is a description of a given situation based on total honesty. You might break down the past day, for example, and pose yourself some hard questions. Did you move too fast? What kinds of choices did you make? Were they for honesty or convenience? Were you true to yourself? The idea is to get beyond reflex, beyond the habitual, to look at things *as if for the first time.* Only through this kind of painful striving can you come to know what is really important to you.

Sometimes a fact check will reveal the blindingly obvious or the patently absurd. If for example, you are always looking for the proper way to ask your son why he's such a slob that he can't find the clothes basket, or to tell your daughter that she's such a dolt she can't open a can without slicing her finger, well, maybe by getting that reality out into the open you can admit that *you are too needling* and that this demand for perfection is what is really making you unhappy. Perhaps then you can change your behavior and tune into harmony instead, saying, "Those are the facts and it doesn't make me happy to dwell on them—so perhaps I'll do what *would* make me happy." Then close the door on his messy room, or buy a can opener she *can* operate.

Fact checking helps discredit common, first-level thoughts such as over-generalizing a problem, distorting details, and jumping to conclusions. Does something always happen to you or only occasionally? Will someone kill you when they find out about an error you've made or just get annoyed? Will you definitely fail to get the promotion because you were late last week, or are you jumping to conclusions? Fact, fact, fact. Nothing is always. A mistake won't kill you. And you probably won't miss a promotion because of one slip-up. Calm down! The exaggeration you live with is very likely taxing your heart, your brain, and your health.

Fact checking is also very helpful in controlling fear. The ultimate goal is to work beyond the fear, and checking the facts can speed up the process and bring your equilibrium back to order. Say you are apprehensive about giving a speech. Is your fear the fear of failure? Of embarrassment? Are you afraid of appearing stupid? If this is your first speech, is it the fear of the unknown, perhaps the possibility of fear that *may yet* arrive? Are you fearful of the physical pain brought on by anxiety, uncontrolled breathing, sweaty palms, or an upset stomach?

Write down some facts about the situation you face. Fact: there are plenty of resources out there to help you. Perhaps you can get yourself a book full of useful anecdotes for warming up a crowd. Maybe there's a course at the community college you can take, or maybe you know a seasoned speaker who can advise you. Now that's fact.

Fact: your fear of incompetence begins and ends with you, or why would you have been selected to give the speech? You may expose the fact that your first impulse is to avoid any kind of personal risk, but having faced this, you will realize that you have met challenges before, that you are bound to do all right, and that even embarrassment is momentary, it is not a reflection of who you really are. Maybe the fact of the matter is that you could stand to join a rotary or speakers' organization and learn the craft of speech delivery, if it's going to be required of you again in the future or if it has become part of the risk for new authority. Factor it out—you'll feel a lot better.

Organize

"Organize" might sound like a generic term, but in this context it takes a specific form, offering a series of steps toward solving a problem or finding an answer. It's main purpose is to slow everything down, not unlike the slowed breathing in yoga, and so the first step is to get yourself in a more relaxed and analytical mood. Take a walk, play the guitar, sing, bake a cake, sketch with colored pencils, read light poetry, or look at a book of cartoons.

After you are sufficiently slowed and you feel a shift from frenetic worry to a *what next?* feeling, you are ready to continue. Turn your journal horizontally, if necessary, and line out six columns or sections. The first will be headed, *Expected.* Write down the anticipated outcome of your problem.

The next column is headed, *Blame.* Here's your chance to vent. Point the finger at all those who are participating in or contributing to the problem.

The next column is *Obstacles.* These include any outside or unforeseen influences that have complicated the problem or that you perceive to be hindering the situation. Next to this, list what you are *Feeling,* emotions that welled up in you at the start of the problem and those collected inside you now.

Now under the heading of *Distance*, try to write out the problem as if it belonged to someone else: My friend is upset because . . . Mentally divorce yourself from the situation and write about it with a shift from the "I" viewpoint to the "he or she" viewpoint.

Your last column will be *Accomplished*, and in it you will focus on the situation or problem and determine what you did right. If you feel you managed to shine through the adversity in some way, how did you do it?

Now that you have organized your perceptions into these six categories, *Expected, Blame, Obstacles, Feelings, Distance*, and *Accomplished*, the next step is to reduce it. Think of your plan as a chair. Four well-balanced legs are all you need to make a seat, correct? All right, then—what shall we get rid of?

Blame would be the best first choice. Though you cannot control what happens to you all the time, you can control your attitude toward it, and blame is a self-defeating and destructive activity. Before you discard it out of hand, however, you might want to figure out what it was that made you feel this way initially. Was it really something that someone else did to you, or can you assume that he did what he thought was fair for himself?

Obstacles needs to be omitted next, because it's superfluous. It was good to release your feelings about the items you listed, but you can't let them stop you. They should be easier to get around if you think of them as negative but illuminating factors you can do nothing about.

Your new four-sided position should provide you with sufficient stability and objective evidence to chart a plan for the solution, resolution, or dissolution of the problem. Even if the solution or answer is one of failure, in your mind, or at least a disappointing outcome, you are closer either to resolving the event or accepting the inevitability of it.

Personality and Self-portrait

The thing that causes people to recognize you after many years of absence and say, "You'll never change" or "You're just the same" has nothing to do with your distinctive hairstyle, your long, thin hands, or even that scar on your forehead from getting hit with a stray ball at age four. It's your personality.

The core traits of your physical style, the arrangement and distinctive pattern of your manner, voice, and speech patterns, all contribute to you, but your innate personal temperament is at the core. No clear winner has yet emerged in the old battle of environment versus heredity, but it is certain that there is a mark of heredity as permanent as the ink in a tattoo that makes people stay true to their personalities. That's why, if you're struggling with an id question or trying to figure out where you fit into a scenario, it's a good idea to learn what it is that defines you. What is your activity level; do you have a propensity to be edgy or easygoing? Are you essentially cheerful or prone to moodiness, even when you're alone? How do you react to the stress of a pressing situation or unexpected change?

By exploring your specific desires and needs along with your personality traits, you can learn a lot that will be useful to you in future writing. Whether you do something as formal as taking a Briggs-Myers personality test, or as simple as keeping track of your preferences, the process should prove enlightening. A book like, *The Personality Self-Portrait* by Oldham and Morris (Bantam) may also be a help.

Questionnaire

In your quest for self-knowledge, a lighter aspect of seeking information is to fill out questionnaires. Questionnaires or quizzes can be found in a variety of periodicals and magazines and range from the absurdly humorous variety to the more thought-provoking life-assessments. Fill these out and paste them, with their score assessments, into your journal.

Quizzes provide a lighthearted avenue for tapping into your thoughts from a new direction. But don't sell them short as completely frivolous or unfounded. One may just turn out to be the key to the next level of thinking and understanding—and no vehicle or method that accomplishes that should be discounted.

Creative Action Checklist

❖ Write a letter to someone for no special reason. If you find yourself writing interesting or revealing things, copy them into your journal.

❖ Make a list of what Chuck Colson has referred to as the Budweiser good life versus the Aristotle good life: that is, success and accomplishment versus virtue and worth.

❖ Do something you don't want to do but that needs doing. Then relax with a friend.

❖ Visit a church in a different neighborhood or attend a festival with an ethnic theme.

Creative Comfort List

❖ Ask yourself, *What did I do with my arms today?* Now find something to do with your arms that will make you feel better—take a whirlpool bath, play billiards, hug a lover.

❖ Get to work early and have the first fresh cup of coffee. Unwind with the shades drawn, read a few pages of a new novel, or just relax without attending to work just yet. Remember, you did arrive early.

❖ Make a promise to yourself to sing or whistle at least one song today.

❖ Have a good non-professional photo taken with your best friend in a nice setting, a park or restaurant. Make two 5 x 7 copies and frame them. Keep one for yourself and give the other to your friend.

Chapter 3

Innerscape

"Stone walls do not a prison make
Nor iron bars a cage."

— RICHARD LOVELACE
To Althea, From Prison

Narrow, first-level thinking, the immediate response to any situation
or event, can do more to hem us in and imprison us than any outside influence. So many people, whether busy at work or occupied
in their own self-imposed hustle, move, operate, and live with con-
viction about what they say and do—without ever having seriously
thought anything through.

The intuitive thoughts, patterns, and instincts that pop into
our heads and compel us spontaneously to wonder can be valuable.
In the words of author and neurologist Richard Restak, the *creative*
process demands "a surrender of logical, everyday modus oper-
andi based on deductions." Creativity is a process that happens without relying on point-A-to-point-B reasoning; it is, by contrast a
process of *surrender*.

There are many instructive and entertaining books on creativity as it relates to business, art, and thought. A list of suggested reading is provided at the end of this book. For now, let us look at a
composite of some of the best techniques for tapping into your own
creative resources. The purpose is to try new mind exercises and directions, and then, along with the information given, to be able to

use these strategies in your journal writing.

Some people would not think twice about skipping the creative exercises. They say, *I can't draw or come up with new ideas. I'm just not creative.* Good news is awaiting those balkers and cynics. They're wrong.

You have, on occasion, been extremely creative, and you didn't think about it twice. There have been times when you have unconsciously pushed the edge, times when you have gone with an inspiration, moments when you have shown faith in your intuition—and you probably didn't even realize or acknowledge it.

Being creative is a simple process of letting go. You give up your preconceived ideas, your strict way of doing things. At first you might look at the process as a shake-up of the ritualistic you, and then you come to realize that it's not that difficult to look at things in a different way. Then there will be a period of openness when you digest the new thinking and tell yourself it's okay to make friends with another side of yourself. Finally, when you can perform the creative exercise freely, almost meditatively, you can fulfill some positive realization: the *Eureka! I've got it!* stage.

For brainstorming solutions to problems, or *path finding*, three approaches are offered. Managerial psychologist Harold J. Leavitt describes the three paths as choices: proactive, reactive, and enactive. You can be proactive and aggressively air and pursue your problems and goals. You can be reactive by passively adjusting to whatever life throws at you. Or you can be enactive and work on a specific problem until you find the right path or solution. When you see the problem and its solution as part of a dialogue between your inner and outer selves, you are being enactive. This is where the creative pictures and bits in your journal can help.

Tapping the Creative Unconscious

All writing techniques in this section are preceded by a few moments of simple relaxation. Begin by sitting up straight and taking deep, cleansing breaths. Sit symmetrically so that your body is well-balanced and nothing is strained, tensed, or cut off. Shake off anxiety by being curious and applying yourself to the task, however silly it may seem at first.

Imagery

Entire books have been devoted to imagery, which is another way of talking about imagination, visualization, or fantasy. You can demystify the concept by doing this first simple set of concentrations. You can work alone or let someone with a soft soothing voice guide you. Close your eyes and picture a familiar object, such as a book. Open it up, turn the pages. Then think about seeing a coffee cup or mug. Look inside to see whether it's full or empty. Picture a telephone. With eyes closed, "view" the front door of the house you've always wanted opening to you.

Let's incorporate sounds into our closed-eyed world. Relax and think about waves rolling in and kissing the seashore. Let that pass and try to hear someone whispering to you. Can you hear bird song, or a high-timbre tone like the ring of a bell? What about the sound of the lawnmower starting up on Saturday morning?

You can taste things in imagery, too. The tartness of a cut lemon can pucker your lips if you touch it with your mind's tongue. The thought of biting into marshmallows or raisins can make your mouth water.

Touch imagery can bring back memories of comfort or irritation. The soft fur behind a cat's ears or the itch of a rough wool sweater are easily called to mind at a suggestion.

With imagination you can span time, taking your mind back to who you were a year ago. You can also use these techniques to propel yourself ahead to rehearse an upcoming speech, practice a song, request a raise, or prepare for any other challenge. Picture yourself entering into a task or commitment and coming off square, with integrity and direction; feel that you have achieved your goal honestly; finally, imagine the glow of success. Such preparation can help you achieve your goals when the time comes to take action.

Now try to transfer some of this imagery onto paper. Knowing that you can control your mind through its senses should help open up a new dimension, a feeling that you can travel anywhere—backward, forward, and into a state of meditative control. You can look on a problem as a daydream and imagine that you have the answer to the situation, even if it seems outlandish at first.

Last but not least, imagery may provide you with the urge for continued writing. Maybe it will spur you on to write for yourself, or others, by using the fiction world in your head to make up fantasy, science fiction, romance, adventure, poetry, or children's stories. Storytelling can be a satisfying natural release and does not have to be "professional" to be enjoyable or valuable.

Cluster

"Clustering" was a landmark technique developed by writer Gabriele Lusser Rico in 1973. (A similar technique was emerging at about the same time in the work of Englishman Tony Buzan, under a process he called "mapping.")

The purpose of clustering is to undercut tension, anxiety, and the natural resistance to writing and expression. In her book called *Writing the Natural Way*, Rico says that when we were children, "wonder was gradually replaced by the complacency of knowing what everyone else knew, of seeing what everyone else saw, and of writing what everyone else wrote."

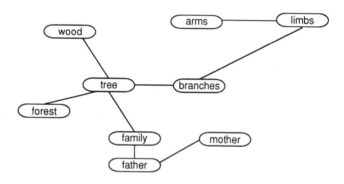

Clusters, also referred to as bubbles, pillows, and clouds, is an easy technique. To begin, a topic word or small phrase is circled in the middle of a fresh sheet of paper. For example, you might put the word "tree" in a centered circle. Now, let your mind build up some loose connections to that word. Jot each one down as it occurs to you and circle it; then connect your new cluster word to the original circle by drawing a line between the two, radiating out in any direction. For the starter word "tree," you might logically, on first-level thinking, come up with the word "branches." *Branches* would then be put in a circle positioned close to the topic word *tree* and a line drawn between the two to connect them. This procedure continues until all the unpressured associations to the word *tree* are exhausted.

Rico's "Design mind's shorthand," as she calls it, forms patterns of ideas and associations rather than sequential thoughts. The free-sketching feeling and non-threatening pattern of mapping your mind's thoughts in small, self-contained vignettes makes it easy to web the small ideas that pop into your head into a larger, more comprehensive whole.

Don't let the clustering device be confined to your journal writing alone. It can be a useful tool for goal planning, for figuring out the small integrated details within large, unwieldy subjects, and it can provide a quick and unrestrained method for writing of all kinds—including reports, themes, speeches, letters, and proposals.

Draw

The *best* reason to draw is that you can't talk intelligibly and draw at the same time. Thus, drawing allows you to get away from the logical, critical-thinking side of you. You put your mind into a freer, less judgmental, dynamic part of your creative mind. Often equated with other activites like dreaming and intuition, a drawing project can prove relaxing, uninhibiting, timeless, and just plain fun.

To begin, find a drawing or even a print of a masterpiece that you are fond of. Set up a blank sheet of paper on a firm surface, and—before you start to copy the original—turn it *upside down*. Of course, your drawing of it will also be upside down! As you work, resist the temptation to turn the picture around in order to see what something is. In fact, refuse to let your brain label whatever part you're working on at any given moment, saying, *that this is a hand, here's an ear*, or whatever. You don't need to know what it is, and you want to avoid talking to yourself in words during the drawing process.

When you are finished, you may be surprised to see how good your drawing actually is. Artist Betty Edwards uses this technique in art classes with students of all ages, as she outlines in her landmark book, *Drawing on the Right Side of the Brain*. Her students are almost always pleased with their upside-down results; they didn't know they were so talented! The shift in this exercise away from critical thinking is akin to taking off on a garden path, away from the highway of rote thinking. The verbal and visual breakaway of drawing things *differently* (upside down) and apart from their usual connections incites new brain stimulation, throwing off one of the roadblocks to creativity.

Dreams

Sleep is a powerful dimension. One ancient story has it that a Chinese philosopher dreamed he was a butterfly dreaming that he was a man. When he awoke, he was not sure whether he was still the butterfly dreaming that he was a man, or a man who had dreamed that was he a butterfly.

There are numerous theories about dreams. The best known is that of Sigmund Freud. He believed that dreams disguised themselves in the form of symbols and had a latent content, that they were a quiet way of demonstrating anxiety.

A more contemporary theory comes from J. Allen Hobson, author of *The Dreaming Brain* and researcher at Harvard University Dream Laboratory. Hobson suggests that dreams mean exactly what they seem to mean. And he says that one of the reasons dreams are not easily "accessible" is that not everybody can handle the intensely emotional, illogical content and organization that characterize the dreaming state. In a sense, then, a dream is a temporary psychosis, and all "major signs of mental illness can be imitated by normal minds in the normal state of dreaming."

Whether you believe that dreams erupt from an unsettled issue pushing into reality or that they are representative icons of something much deeper, you will still agree that if a recurring dream seems to hold some intuition, it would be wise not to ignore it. How to remember dreams is the next question. For although you may claim not to dream at all, or not to be able to remember your dreams afterward, there are ways of trapping these elusive night visions.

Preparation is essential. Have paper and pencil ready and within easy reach. The night before, ask for dreams. *I will remember my dreams.* You may even try to program what you dream by asking a question over and over in your mind as a mantra or repetitive phrase. You can eventually lull yourself to sleep in this manner. Relax, breathe deeply, and anticipate remembering what you dream as you drift away from consciousness.

Christina Baldwin, author of *One to One*, says she sometimes sets her alarm to go off forty-five minutes early in the hopes of catching her dream mid-way. When you wish to catch a recent dream, move slowly as you awake so as not to jar the dream out of your mind. As you begin to reconstruct the images from whatever point you remember, do so gently and without much extraneous activity. Only by thinking about dreams and writing them down will you return them to conscious memory.

Now, you say, *what do I do with my dream?* Think about what it may be trying to tell you. Look at or draw the images and see whether they relate to what is happening in your life. Use some free association by reiterating the events or symbols in the dream and see whether anything unusual or telling comes to the paper. Is it possible to transform your dream into a poem that will help you to take charge of confused feelings?

If you can change the viewpoint of the characters in your dream, that may give you a new perspective. Do you sense any personal vulnerability in rereading your notes? Read them aloud and ask this question again. If you are feeling inhibited with the interpretation phase, you can repeat the process with a week's worth of dream notes, organizing them into a *list of main themes.*

A most beautiful and creative technique is practiced by the Senoi Indians of Malaysia. Their dreams are considered to have an important relationship to their waking lives. They share their dreams daily, consider them when making decisions, and receive helpful observations from their elders on the directions that a heroic or creative dream might bring.

You may want to recreate your dream using imagery. Perhaps you can give yourself a second chance to affect the outcome of a dream. Take more control of your thoughts by using a daydream, or as Baldwin calls it, "creative tripping." By this process, you can begin to imagine new capabilities for yourself, and later, foster more inner dialogue during the one-third of your life that slips by in sleep.

A famous teacher and diarist of the "intensive journal," Ira Progoff, believed that one could construct a fantasy at will and that your options for decision making were wrapped up in invention. By allowing yourself to *imagine life as it would be if the opposite direction had been made,* and by stepping into that fantasy, Progoff believed you would be led to make new and better decisions.

New Edges

New edges is taking a thing as far as it will go in any direction. It has to do with new awareness of limits: from far to near, first to last, soft to loud, up to down, outside to inside, and so on. The idea is to take a problem or idea to its furthest boundaries, to the absurd on either end, and find the answer somewhere in between.

A normal reaction to a problem is to avoid it. You're going to do the opposite. After stating the problem or question in a main heading, you're going to pilot right into it and find its outer limits. First write down, *What is the worst possible thing that can happen from this problem?* Use your senses to their fullest and come up with the worst possible scenario.

On the other end of the scale, write, *What's the best possible thing that can come from this situation?* Try to assess the situation as honestly as you can, because your mind will want to tell you that nothing good can come from your problem.

Now dealing with extreme opposites always, try to imagine yourself an impartial investigator for the New Edges Task Force and ask yourself, *What is the absolute first thing to do?* Then ask, *What is the last thing that I can do?*

You may find it helpful to approach the problem from another viewpoint, *What does this look like to those not involved?* And its opposite, *How is this for the insiders; what are they feeling?*

Perhaps you are worrying (unproductive reaction), or trying to overcontrol (over-active action) the environment, the people, their feelings, and the things involved. Try to see the larger picture by exaggerating its boundaries.

Rank the steps you need to take to solve the problem or outline the goal and list them from pleasant to least pleasant. Or from least pleasant to most pleasant. Figure out whether there is a way to make what you need to do enjoyable. For example, perhaps you can reward yourself for doing the least pleasant task first. If you have procrastinated, just taking that first step and getting it out of the way—making that phone call, tackling the decision early, or going ahead with the test—may be its own reward, but you might want to do something more substantial to celebrate.

There are so many mixed messages today that ideas once considered cast in stone are no longer reliable. With the new edges technique, you will be circumventing mixed messages by taking a situation to the extreme boundaries of absurdity, so that your own common sense will provide you with prudent answers. You will face the deal head-on and locate the middle ground. Give your final decision your total attention, and then let go.

Dictionary

The dictionary device is probably the easiest to reject out of hand, since its success hinges on a combination of prior knowledge and serendipity. Serendipity is chance, good fortune, a godsend, or a random stroke of good luck, but this very randomness provides creative freedom from tension and from the anxiety of making the correct decision.

In this method, sometimes referred to as the "aleatory" method, words are plucked at hazard from a dictionary and a connection construed to shed new light on the problem. The word *aleatory* is derived from the Latin words for *dice* and *dice player*, and the premise of the procedure is that the writer or problem solver will not consciously engineer the direction of his or her thoughts for any set purpose but will accept what comes like a roll of the dice.

You need to have faith that a shift from logical thinking to unstructured chaos will lend itself to opportunity. Haven't we all heard stories of completely unrelated ideas coming together to form new thoughts and solutions? A great many inventions were discovered not as a result of a methodical search from one method to another in the lab but through the random, happenstance association of one seemingly unrelated event to another. For example, what possible use could be made of burrs clinging to your clothes as you walk through the woods? What idea could those irritating little prickers give rise to? Answer: Velcro®. So don't be too skeptical.

Close your eyes and run your finger down dictionary lists on various pages, selecting a few words at random. Write them on your paper and see what you come up with. Eureka!

Free Association

If you like to let your mind wander, free association is for you; at the very least it encourages mental exploration. The two basics of free association are anchored by "nothings"—have nothing in particular in mind when you sit down to write, and remember that nothing is insignificant when it pours out of you.

The method you bring to free association is surrealist in nature, as you race to take down the thoughts that flow from a relaxed, empty mind. The only prerequisite for using free association will be a sense of a *need* to write, a longing, if you will.

The spontaneity of this exercise may seem silly or embarrassing to you, but in fact it can be quite enjoyable. When you reach pure involvement, you are so much in sync with the present moment that your state is one of total distraction. Like a pot coming to boil, you are allowing thoughts to rise up to the surface.

Since this technique is meant to foster the uninhibited play of pen on paper, give yourself plenty of room. That way, if you change direction, scribble in sketches or doodles, switch the pen to your other hand, or decide to write on different levels, you'll have the space to do so.

There are no rules to free association. If you need a trigger to get you started, you can use the word "I," start with a question or a statement, or borrow a starter word like "special," "mother," "real," or "time." Results may be unexpected, and unanticipated connections may seem puzzling, confusing, or even scary to you at first. It may help you to reread and think about your writing in the same frame of mind and with the same reference as it was written.

Most people turn to journal writing during a time of crisis or when they need a plan to reorganize. Free association is for the other times—when the goal is simply self-exploration for its own sake.

Creative Problem Solving

Creative problem solving is not one thing but a series of creative treatments that you apply to your life to make something work.

A Kentucky woman named Joyce Case stopped the lose-regain again cycle of dieting by keeping a journal. She says that each of her numerous diet attempts was sabotaged by some emotionally traumatic event. That event could be as minor as a broken fingernail or as major as the death of her mother.

On her fiftieth birthday Case looked at all the times diets had failed her and tried to figure out why she could not keep the weight off. She also made an effort to examine the pros and cons of trying one last diet. This careful study and a new sense of determination made her decide to keep a daily journal. It was not, as Joyce says, "a diet diary, not a journal of my weight-loss progress or eating problems, but a journal to keep me emotionally on track. I simply write about what is happening in my life, good or bad. I write out my anger, my frustration, my unhappiness. Before, when I felt miserable, I'd eat and cry and stare out the window wondering why I felt that way."

Joyce told *Prevention* (October 1989) that she would write as if she were talking to her best friend, a supportive friend who would not judge her. Her friend was the thin and confident person inside her. And apparently this creative problem solving has worked for Joyce, who is now 100 pounds lighter after realizing her one-and-a-half-year goal. Her husband has since had triple bypass surgery, something that would, in the past, as Joyce says, "have blown me and my diet away." Her handle on stress and diet is in her daily journal.

Three creative writing/drawing techniques to use as emotional stress modifiers were developed by Michael Ray and Rochelle Myers in their book, *Creativity in Business*. The techniques are left-hand/right-hand, mandalas, and hieroglyphics.

Left-Hand/Right-Hand. Left-Hand/Right-Hand is an exercise employed to encourage responses from the lesser-used side of your brain. Write out a question or a problem but don't try to puzzle out an answer. Emphasize to yourself that the answer lies within you but that it will be written out by your less-dominant hand. Then let the opposite hand record your mind's answer. Any surprises?

Mandalas. The word *mandala* comes from Sanskrit, a classical language of the Hindu peoples, and it means both circle *and* center. Mandalas occur in Christian and Judaic religious traditions, in yoga disciplines, and as art shapes appearing in Aztec, Tibetan, and Indian cultures. Throughout history, mandalas have been known to symbolize eternal opposites, such as mortal and immortal, masculine and feminine, Yin and Yang. The shapes within the circle can be representative of both hard and soft, eternal and transient.

Three elements of the mandala are the circle's center (the point from which the compass circle is set), the symmetry (the area surrounding), and its cardinal points (directionals). The center of

the circle remains as a constant, the symmetry represents the drawings that surround the center, and the north, south, east, and west in the circle's radius are its cardinal points.

The center of your mandala can represent the "I am" or heart point of your circle, and the drawings you make within its borders can radiate out from the heart point or flow within. Your drawing can include colors, shapes and non-representative forms, all within the body of the circle. It is supposed to be meditative and relaxing, and the interpretation is up to you.

Mandalas were practiced by Stanford University business students under the tutelage of Ray and Myers, who used the results in a study course and later, their book. They report that students often used mandalas to help deal with a difficult situation, such as discovering their true feelings about a trauma.

For mandalas, a circle is drawn with a compass. Colored pens, pencils, or crayons are used to make flow drawings within the circle. Music may be incorporated as an aid to your process but the main feeling is to think meditatively, in a relaxed breathing state, eyes closed initially and then to concentrate on letting the center of the mandala become the center of your existence.

Symbols. An interesting and definitive creative technique for problem-solving is the use of *symbols.* An entire line of icons or small pictures are laid in a row. Images of ancient Egyptian hieroglyphs can be drawn out, but a simpler tack would be to use a set of tarot

cards or even a set of children's picture flash cards. Lay out a row of about ten to twelve symbols. Concentrate on a problem or question in your life and write it down in your journal. With your eyes closed, do a relaxation exercise such as deep breathing, and when you open your eyes, write down what the pictures are telling you about your present situation.

New Direction

Role-play by taking on the guise of listener/advisor. If you were to assume the position of an advice columnist for a famous newspaper, what would be your response to a letter from someone facing the situation you are struggling with now? For years people have relied on the advice of complete strangers in just this way. Why? Because it is advice untempered by emotion, unfettered by worry, and entirely objective. The answers given are based on common sense, not personal involvement. Good old traditional wisdom, courtesy, good taste, and moral ethics are within you, too. Assume the role creatively: "Dear Editor-in-Charge of Self . . ."

Creative Action Checklist

- ❖ Where is a place you used to go often besides the place where you work? Plan to go there tonight. Who are the people there?

- ❖ Have a friend or another couple over for pinochle, charades, or interactive games.

- ❖ If your child has friends of a different ethnic group or culture, arrange a get-together with their parents.

Creative Comfort List

- ❖ What is something that you made this year that you really enjoyed? Whether it was cooking a new food, creating something arts and craftsy, or building a deck, ask yourself why you did it and how did you feel after? Congratulate yourself for tackling something new, and plan something else.

- ❖ Have your favorite comfortable outfit cleaned and wear it anywhere.

❖ Do something involving water; listen to a waterfall, go to the pool, walk in a warm rain, enjoy a hot tub with a friend.

❖ Leave your family and friends humorous, sexy, and loving post-it notes all over the house.

Chapter 4

Journal Self-Esteem

"We are all born mad. Some remain so."
— SAMUEL BECKETT

The fact that life is full of problems is often hard to accept. No, scratch that—problems are a *grind*, a real grind. In fact, many people can never fully bring themselves to do what they need to do about their problems, often going to great lengths—alcohol, drugs, or other numbing behavior—to avoid the pain and confrontation involved in solving their problems.

Many sufferers are convinced that their difficulties must be unique to them, their families, their culture, or their race. The exhausting and sometimes elaborate process of not dealing with their problems shows up in the most effective and debilitating form it can: stress.

Lou Harris, the public polling expert, says in his book *Inside America* that a substantial 89 percent of all adult Americans (158 million people) report experiencing high stress. Of these, fully more than half, 59 percent say they feel "great stress" at least once or twice a week.

Stress means tension, anxiety, and nervousness. A quarter of all stressed-out people report headaches; others talk of anger and irritability with co-workers and family. Symptoms lead to fatigue, depression, and poor consequences for overall health.

Take your coping seriously; repressed feelings can make you

sick. In a forty-one-year study of 1,337 students conducted at Johns Hopkins University, psychologists found out that those who held in tension at age twenty were twice as likely to die by age fifty-five as peers who expressed their anxieties or felt little tension (*USA Today*, August 20, 1991).

With men, stress can be an old-fashioned by-product of leading secret emotional lives. From an early age, most men consciously or unconsciously learn to hide away their deepest fears and insecurities. Psychologist Daniel Weinberger at Case Western Reserve University in Cleveland says a study of 48 sixth-grade boys found that half the boys were defensive and shunned emotional expression. A third of the defensive group had asthma; none in the other group. Also, the mothers of the children in the less-expressive boy's group reported that their children had significantly more aches and pains.

Weinberger also found, through a study involving 179 grown men, that those who were suppressing hostility and aggression had a higher LDL (bad cholesterol).

People's feelings are like onions: many layers deep. Motivational books can help stimulate people to change, but unfortunately the benefits often wear off quickly. That is the great advantage of journal keeping. It's a discipline that not only uncovers the first-level realizations but cuts much deeper over time. Because the resulting self-revelations are discovered on your own, not generated by others, they are more profound, simply because they originate and end with the writer. Self-discovery can lead to better coping skills and give you a new sense of personal direction. You'll begin doing things not because someone tells you to but because you uncover what's truth for you.

All our lives we are taught to put walls around our true thoughts, questions, and desires. We are put into gender roles as children: "big boys don't cry" or "little girls don't talk like that." We are manipulated into behaviors by guilt, or humiliation, in the name of religion, in the name of decency, for the sake of our parents, and "for our own good."

Meditative thinking and change come from confronting suffering and pain, and writing is a fundamental vehicle for that. Treat journal writing like mental yoga—a cleansing stretch and posture to keep the mind young, healthy, and agile.

Venting, Realizing, and Coping

Because the goals explored in this chapter are emotional ones, it will differ somewhat from the rest of the book in that the techniques offered will be introduced side-by-side with certain emotional conditions. It offers tailor-made tools and formats to cope with the emotions described, but this does not mean that the techniques are not interchangeable; they can be. If someone with a "poor image" feels uncomfortable using the device *exaggerated judgment*, she may prefer to express her feelings through a written *dialogue* between herself and her childhood self. Anger can be sorted out and redirected by taking advantage of the *unsent letter* technique, or perhaps a *self-esteem assessment* is what you need to diffuse your envy-driven anger.

Anxiety

Stress, anxiety, and worry are a threesome. Buy into one, you often get all three. They always come to a crisis together. We've seen that stress and its relations are the physical symptoms of not dealing with problems. Anxiety is a second cousin to stress and can be called the fear or dread of something unknown. Anxiety can be a powerful emotion, because most of your energy goes into resisting conscious awareness of your problem, leaving you depleted and listless. If you are depressed, unable to sleep, sleeping too much, or suffering from other unwanted behaviors, worry may be the hidden cause. Stress and anxiety exert their influence in turn and need to be booted out.

Candle Concentration. This exercise can relieve the symptoms of anxiety by giving you something else to focus on. Sit at a cleared table with a lit candle placed a comfortable distance away. Take a few deep breaths, gazing into the flame of the candle. Let the impression of the flame burn itself onto your retinas for a minute or two (this will not hurt them). Then, slowly and deliberately, bring your hands up to your eyes and gently place your palms, the fleshy part just above your wrists, over your eyes so they fit like a blinder—not squeezing or pressing, just gently blocking the light.

If you are not pressing too hard, you will see the flame's image in the back of your mind. The background will be very black and the candle flame will burn brightly. If the flame you see has a tendency to rise, you can manipulate the flame and keep it in a level line. The color of the flame will gradually fade from bright yellow, taking on an aura of blue, green, or red. Stay with the image until it disappears from your mind.

This five-to-ten-minute exercise is powerfully calming, a benefit that cannot be undervalued when you are feeling anxious. Tranquility may bring a state of restfulness or a mind prepared to think about choice. There is power in non-anxious choice. With controlled choice you have decided to take charge of how you feel.

Do Something Different. After slowing biological indicators such as heart rate and breathing, and getting rid of that stress headache, you can now make a list of things that can be done—and pick something from the list that can be done *immediately.*

Maybe your first choice is to change your location. A change of venue can deflate anxiety by forcing you to pay attention to your new surroundings instead of worries. You can go to a museum and wrap yourself in art; or, you can choose to do something physically active and useful, like washing the car, brushing the dog, or digging in the garden. All these can take your mind off anxiety—distract it long enough to get you back to normal. In your renewed state of composure, think about looking for journal answers or a further change in perception.

Please note that in the case of acute anxiety, where none of the above methods succeed in alleviating symptoms, the next step may be to seek professional advice to reduce anxiety.

Worry

Mary McClure Goulding, a psychotherapist and coauthor of the book *Not to Worry*, says, "Worry is only useful for the certain amount of time it takes you to decide what you're going to do to make the worry not come true." For example, if your worry is keeping you up at night, the time is well spent if it leads you to rewrite that under-researched proposal you skimped on, make an apology that's eating at you, or make you decide to get a breast exam; if, that is, worry does not preclude action. The time is not well spent if you are worrying about hypothetical dangers or problems over which you have no control. *"What if I get sick? What if the roof falls in?"* (Of course, if you think there's any danger of that, then do something!)

Unsent Letters. There are a lot of old-school preconceptions surrounding worry. Write a letter to your worry: "Dear Worry . . ." In the letter, try to determine why you worry. Do you feel that by worrying you could be avoiding bad news? Is it an excuse not to think about something else? Is there superstition in your worrying; do you secretly believe that if you worry about something, it's less likely to happen?

Tell worry in your letter that you are not going to try to resist it. Chances are, if you try not to think about the problem, your unwanted thoughts will only keep reappearing until they occupy center stage.

Stare It in the Face. If, instead, you accept your worry, you can desensitize yourself to it by allotting it a specific chunk of time. To give a specific worry your full concentration, set aside the same time every day, say a half-hour period when you are free from distractions, interruptions, and outside influences, and jot down notes. You'll want to end your worry period with a plan of action.

In a study conducted by Elwood Robinson, a psychology professor, distraught subjects were told to do nothing but worry for a full thirty minutes. Many found this a daunting task and ". . . maxed out after ten or fifteen minutes," he says (*Health* July/August 1992).

Job Burnout

With a large portion of our lives devoted to working, job burnout is a common problem. The term *burnout* was coined over 22 years ago by a psychologist named Herbert J. Freudenberger. What he was referring to was a feeling of depletion that preys on your energy, strength, and resources, a syndrome that occurs over a period of months and years. Perfectionism, work overload, nonstop stress, and a fear of getting fired can all contribute.

Freudenberger believed that as many as one in four people end up burning out in his or her job. Job burnout signals, in addition to the physical symptoms of stress, can include irritability, an overtly critical attitude, and an inability to concentrate.

Business disappointment, fueled by misconceptions and faulty

expectations, often prompts job burnout. If your long-term ambitions seem to be defeated by your daily struggle for success, or if you
feel as if you are chasing money and always trying to "make it," you
may be headed for burnout.

Key Words. Since these kinds of job frustrations develop over a
period of time, they will not be wiped out just because you notice
them. The first strategy is to believe that control resides in you.
Make some lists of *key words* to help you. For instance, you could list
the best words to use in communicating your desires to a boss who
is constantly giving you unrealistic deadlines. Be specific in your
needs, because you must be able to translate your problems into
some viable action or condition. For example, if you need time to
visit your child's teacher, or you want to ask for a personal hour during the day (in exchange for coming in earlier or staying later), the
extra preparation time spent getting your emotions in check and
sorting out your thoughts can enable you to talk calmly and honestly about what it is you really want. Remember to use a key word
term like "negotiate" instead of "demand" or "need," and define
what your request means to you and to your company.

Make another key word list of what's positive about your job. Include the things you actually enjoy about what you do. For example:

* *Input:* Does your position make you feel as if your input
  counts?

* *Coworkers:* Do you like your relationships with coworkers;
  have they added value to your life?

* *Benefits:* Can you count on medical support?

Think about becoming more involved in what it is that you enjoy the most. Would your personality and leadership skills allow you
to be a good instructor in the training department? Do you have a
flair for organizing board meetings? Find your niche.

Reprioritize. Write down what you assumed your role would be,
what your actual understanding of the job is, and whether this jives
with company policy. Is it possible that you need to set boundaries
and actually say "No" to solving all department problems? Perhaps
you need to redefine what your work goals are. Or perhaps you just

need a change of scene: it could be time to take a vacation, work out a sabbatical arrangement, or fax your work from home. Define your needs.

Look at Expectations. Are you feeling sorry for yourself because you think you have done everything right, to no avail? Did you believe that wanting it all was enough to make it happen? Did you set such unrealistic expectations that you put off living until you become richer, higher up, more mobile? Honestly, did you think for one minute that you could fix the problem with compulsive buying, extra perks, or a temporary high?

Do a Word Portrait. Remember the exercise in chapter 2? This time, pick a highly successful person in your field. Remind yourself that your successful person has his or her own struggles. Maybe you could picture him sitting on a toilet, diapering a screaming child, or talking to himself. No one need ever know about your method of getting in touch with reality. Draw a sketch of this successful person and try to determine whether his clothes, trinkets, or image gives him status. Try to realize that everyone has problems, and name them.

Make Lists. Have you lost sight of yourself? List what it was you wanted to contribute. Do you have a goal not realized? Write it down. Then there's the hardest list of all, the one you make when you have tried all the other techniques to no good result—the "know when to call it quits" list.

What Holds You Back? Perhaps you are repressing your ambition because of fear of failure. Do you often find yourself envious of others' accomplishments; do you picture yourself in their shoes? Does something keep you from networking or from meeting the key players in the company? Do you find the idea of risk taking an ever-pressing problem that looks a lot like avoidance, or do you blame the recession or office politics for your position and status?

There will be more about risk taking in chapter 5, but for now, a primary target for journal writing could be outlining your fear of failing, if that is your problem. Try to define the pros and cons of competing for a better position. Perhaps this will lead you to discuss your conclusions with trusted colleagues and mentors. Weigh what they have told you about their experiences against the gnawing desires that you have for yourself.

Be Realistic. Draw up a *realistic list.* Outline your fantasy about what a new desired level of work would be like, along with what real obstacles and challenges you can anticipate. Do not delude yourself. Is it possible that you want, instead, to drop off the fast-track by choice? What will you channel your new ambitions and intentions into—and can you be realistic about them? These are all good questions to consider as you reevaluate your career, fears, and ambitions.

Fear

If anxiety is the dread of something unknown, then we can safely say that fear is knowing what we dread. Fear is temporary, although it may come more often than we'd like. When it becomes a persistent dread of a particular object or situation, however, it is called a *phobia.* Phobias are very dangerous to your well-being, with the potential to depress your immune system and damage your ability to feel well physically. A true phobia calls for desensitization and the efforts of a psychologist.

Time Reference. Fear, though less dangerous than a phobia, can still be a powerful force, compelling you to behave in a certain way or inhibiting your behavior. Fear is a complicated dish, but a good way to analyze it is to create a *time reference.* Single out your fear by writing down first, in a heading, what it is exactly that you fear. Then answer these questions. Have you had this fear before? How did you handle it in that past? What was the result of your previous experience? Could it be influencing the way you feel now? Honesty and self-knowledge are important first steps in figuring out how to deal with a fear problem.

Stories. Tell yourself that you will not be passive about fear, that you can take steps to control it. Outline or list what those steps could be. Free-associate or cluster your choices; you can always eliminate the wild or unrealistic solutions. The important part of the process is to discover what it is you are afraid of, or afraid to say. Is this a secret you find difficult to admit to yourself, that has perhaps metamorphosed itself into a monster of fear and dread? Produce a *story*, describing and/or drawing your dragon of dread. Then slay it—or tame it—right there on the paper in your journal. Make a grand symbolic ritual of taking up the sword of control.

Perhaps you're afraid of the neighbor's dog, Cujo. In your story, call him Cujinski, and make a list of things to lull the beast, like milkbones or a female dog. Take him for a walk, give him his dinner, or have him lie passively at your feet by your armchair near the fire. Oh yes—chase him off the seat cushion first!

If you are afraid of an upcoming event, make a "movie" of your future actions, rehearsing your behavior so you will not feel like the unprepared actor without a script at an audition.

Banish Childhood Labels. Perhaps your fear is grounded in the way you were brought up or the way your parents labeled your child-like behaviors. In your journal, ask yourself whether you are able to separate what you are from what you do. Can you forgive yourself small childhood digressions, or have you incorporated the cruel labels of "lughead," "slob," "fatso," "dense," "clumsy," or "loser"? Are you in a state of fear or defiance about becoming that name? Have you personalized childhood criticisms, or are they getting in the way of who you really can be?

Write down the *key word* "change." Does change frighten you? How? What does change look like? Sometimes the fear of change is actually the mask of what you think is security. You hide behind whatever it is that makes you feel secure—an image, a status symbol, a dead-end job, a poor characteristic—because it is the nonconfrontational, the easier way to go. Maybe you've worn this image for so long it's become second nature to you, like a familiar face. If you draw a picture of change for yourself, will it help you to shake its influence?

Ugly fear is also linked to another "ugly" guilt. Did your parents have the same religion and personal values, or did you get mixed messages about what a good person and a bad person were? Make a heading, *Childhood Values,* and recall what your father said a good person was. His bad person was lazy, cowardly, a "bum," do you remember? Mother said a bad person was a drinker who broke things, was lazy and said bad things. Jot down all the things your parents told you about the good and the bad. Are your lists and values the same? Do they sit well with you? Have you been afraid to admit that their values are not yours, that they are strange ideas, to your thinking?

Anger

If your fear has turned into anger or hostility, you may want to try some auxiliary things to shake it up.

Diffuse Hostility. According to Dr. Redford Williams at Duke University, a few ways to do this are:

* Incorporate more religion into your life
* Smile (try the molar-revealing grins)
* Do one thing at a time
* Recall pleasant memories and listen to calming or classical music (at least fifteen minutes' worth a day)
* Note your angry feelings on paper every day, and at the end of the week, ask yourself whether it was worth it

When the weekend rolls around, write "I forgive" on a fresh page in your journal and see where it takes you.

Master Anger. Anger is often the result of what we perceive as an insult or injury to ourselves. It can also be the result of something *we* did or failed to do. Is the feeling of anger bad or wrong? Given that anger is a very human emotion, any passion of this nature can be said to have both a worth and a risk. But in your journal writing, some questions need to be answered about anger before it can be thought of in constructive terms.

When you get angry, try to calm yourself by any manner most comfortable to you, such as a temporary distraction or vigorous exercise. Head off the desire to vent your anger on another or even strike back. Telling another person off or spilling your story to an innocent listener can make you feel first angrier and later guilty.

Now, in your writing, *ask* yourself whether the perceived slight was done "on purpose." This is an important consideration. Try to assess the intent. By constructively looking for the cause of the provocation, you are taking steps to effect change, which in turn, will give you some control.

Next, *describe* what you feel. Describe what you see. Could it be that a defensive pride or desire to save face is involved in this situation? Or is this a principle negotiation? Perhaps this is a transfer of anger. Could you be pushing an issue because of something you would rather not face, and are you actually angry about something else altogether? For any legitimate resolve you are best served by identifying the real issue. What, if any, are the underlying interests here?

How can you restore courtesy? *List* ways to do this. Although this may be difficult initially, avoid a contest of wills. You don't need to take a 360-degree turn or "give in" against your instincts, but make sure you are not confusing accomplishing something positive with one-upmanship and a desire to control.

Once the problem or conflict has been identified, try to write down a wide range of possible solutions. Be imaginative. If you look for options, however absurd, the answer may emerge of its own accord. Decide what needs to be done and then write down ways to implement it.

Before you leave your journal, take time for introspection and self-knowledge and write down what your style has been. How do you habitually deal with disputes? By avoidance? Competition? Do you slip into putting the other person down or by trying to make them feel foolish? It could be that you were never taught acceptable responses. In the book *Bringing Up a Moral Child*, Michael Schulman and Eva Mekler advise teaching your child about the realities of everyday life, such as, there will be times when we cannot have what we want because someone else has equal claim to it, or because it will infringe on the rights or well-being of others.

Finally, if your anger cannot be separated from aggression, seek outside help, a counselor or a neutral party. Ignoring a problem could lead to intensified anger, spill over into your work life, create rifts between people, and lead to physical violence.

Negative Judgment

The man who said, "I don't want to belong to any club that would accept me as a member" did not have a poor self-image. In fact, Groucho Marx had one of the most thriving, and perhaps one of the most enthusiastic, egos in history.

If only you and I could say the same! Our own self-esteem is as delicate as a rose, and the fragile balance between our body and mind is open to pummeling by cruel and unobjective comparisons between ourselves and other people. Who is inflicting these exaggerated negative judgments on us? We are—on ourselves.

The little voice chattering on and on inside your head is quite willing to tell you what is wrong with you, why you can't do something, and why you should give up, remain small, or act depressed. Judgment by its very nature is mean and exaggerated. Everything that is wrong with you is bigger than life itself. Judgment is always ready to spill its guts about how dumb you are, what a failure you are—all the while grooming itself for its next attack inside your very own head.

Fight back. Don't allow the negative little creep in your mind to define who you are or measure your worth. *List* how you feel about the negative thoughts that return into your mind and mentally punch them out. Tell them to scat! *Have a conversation with Judgment* and tell him (or her) what you can like about yourself, what you have overcome that makes you special, and why you are not like your judgment's negative thoughts.

Squaring Up. Set up two columns in your journal. The first will represent your commitment to do only what you approve of—you are stating your own value system now. It could include a protest against some unfairness in your life or work, or the promise that you'll actually make a decision when your wife asks you where you want to eat, or a resolve to pay back the money you owe. You can call this column "Squaring Up" or "Starting Over." Through this process you can begin to settle ethical dilemmas—not by rolling over but by learning and exerting your own moral code. This will clean the spare room for integrity and self-esteem.

In the second column, write what you accept about yourself and what that means to you. Are you a valuable family member, a loving father, a patient woman? Can you take a bad situation and turn it in a new direction with your glass-half-full thinking? Write it down.

Self-Portrait. Affirming personal strengths is one thing, but do you know in your heart, and on your medical chart, that you are not caring for yourself enough? Have you neglected giving yourself strokes because you thought you weren't worthy or hadn't earned time for yourself? Have you accepted your womanly shape and personal physiology, or are you still beating yourself up for the image in your mirror?

Writing a respectful *self-portrait* is a valuable tool in the search for an objective viewpoint as you sort out your feelings, negative or otherwise. So is a *word portrait* of someone else, which can act as a projection or mirror on your own personality. You may well be seeing your own positive or negative qualities in another. You didn't realize what it was that drove you crazy about a friend or lover until it dawned on you that it was the very thing you do not like about yourself.

If your portrait of another is unrealistic, if it serves to blind you to who that other person really is, or if you are under a delusion that makes you think that person's life is easier than yours, that is envy. Begin again, and this time do not let infatuation guide your thoughts or writing.

What did you learn?

Pain and Illness

Pain is a fact of life. As neurologist Russell Martin says in *Matters Gray and White*, "It is cruel and calamitous and often constant, and, as its Latin root *poena* implies, it is the corporeal *punishment* each of us ultimately suffers for being alive." There they go, illness and pain, walking hand in hand on their destructive way. You were going your own way, until they randomly intercepted you.

How do you react? Generally, devastated. The "Why me?" syndrome sets in. Are you being punished? Words like "horrible," "the worst," and "calamity" resonate in your head. Why is God letting this happen? Your family suffers for you too, but finds your state obsessive to the point where you are like a glitch in a poor recording, repeating, repeating.

There is no dignity in illness. Life and illness are now the pits into which you were thrown. And if there is uncertainty along with pain and illness, such as not knowing what your prognosis is, your coping strategies are obliterated. On the other hand, if one more person tells you about their "coping story" you'll commit murder, and no one would blame you.

Can you neutralize pain by writing about it? Probably not. And if your parents handled major and minor problems badly, you will be predisposed to do the same. But if you want to change that, if you want to break out of the circle of suffering and endure the symptoms better, you can try self-therapy.

Make a Declaration. The first response to suffering and the most difficult to shuck is the *Why me?* question. There is no answer to it. Reiterating that futile strain over and over, personalizing your pain, as it were, only adds to your distress. Self-persecution and punishment are not the purpose here, unless you want to give glory to grief. So on a new page of your journal, *declare* that you will not ask "Why?" any longer.

Later, if you need to *list* your complaints about illness or pain, do that on a fresh sheet of paper. Next, decide what action you will take against your condition—and burn the rest. Yes, do what you can with drugs, therapy, accupuncture, distraction, and so on, and then take your unresolved complaints and burn them to ashes with a match.

A Time to Look Within. Some people are afraid to change, even in pain, but when you realize that conflict, tension, and confusion are a non-negotiable part of the process, you can avert some of the suffering by trying a new tack. At the very least it will give you a sense of control—the very thing the indignity of illness has threatened to take from you.

Here are some things to ponder as you write in your journal. First, think back to a situation you thought you would never overcome. How did you handle it? How do you feel about it now?

To make sense of what is happening to you, or to bring order to it, discover what message could be encoded in it. You could ask, what am I learning from suffering? The answer may not make itself clear right away, if you are still obsessed with the why and how. But ask again, and continue to ask it periodically. Have you coped with disasters in the past? How did they change you?

Is it possible that pain has its advantages? It does slow you down, take you out of the bustling mainstream and all its denials. Pain and illness force us to let go of the trivial, the mundane, the insignificant. The small and unnoticed now take on new meaning. Suffering can thus serve to bring life into new focus.

Has your capacity for empathy been increased, and will this heightened insight provide new avenues or untapped possibilities for you? Most definitely. You may resist seeing what you're going through as a life-altering discipline when you're in the clutches of pain, but pain does open doors. People change when the message of their illness is discovered. As Rev. Edward B. Pritchard of the Washington Archdiocese says, "suffering transforms the takers to givers."

The way you respond to a serious illness says a great deal about you and your character. Anybody can do well and thrive when things are going right. It's the best in you that copes, changes gears, listens, acknowledges, and channels your needs to a higher plane in times of great struggle.

Treating the Pain. There are some things you can do to alleviate pain. Medication can certainly help, but as Diane Ackerman writes in her book, *A Natural History of the Senses,* "Continuous use of any analgesic can neutralize its beneficial effect, but only twenty minutes of aerobic exercise is enough to stimulate the body to produce more endorphins, natural painkillers. Shifting your attention to something else will distract you from pain; pain requires our full attention. A simple and effective form of pain relief comes from 'lateral inhibition' . . . . [For example,] if you apply ice to a bruise, it will not only help with the swelling, it will also transmit cold messages instead of pain messages" [to your brain].

What else can help? Relaxation techniques and hypnosis can fool the body, stimulate production of endorphins, and change the course of the pain message. Take a few minutes to imagine and describe yourself as healthy, feeling well. Write in your journal (you can also draw a picture) about what health represents. One patient closed his eyes often during the course of his illness and imagined knights in white armor riding white horses and carrying bows and arrows riding through his bloodstream to the place where his tumor was located. At his command the medieval army would attack the cancer and shoot it down.

Coping. Support groups do help. Dr. David Speigel of Stanford Medical School conducted a study of women with breast cancer. Those who participated in support groups, according to his report, lived twice as long as comparable women in no group. His new study on the success of the four longest-term survivors finds that they draw on intense support from at least a few others and that they "all have a quiet determination." (*USA Today*, August 1991.) People confined to bed for long periods can *create alternate worlds* in their journal using news clippings, photos, and world reports. A woman recuperating from jaw surgery, her mouth wired shut for a couple of months, discovered that writing a story of the daily activity of her family around her provided an outlet for the pain.

You can use *distancing* to your advantage by reading self-help books or biographies of others. Inspiration from an objective source is sometimes very comforting. Or, if you are just bored with being laid up, collect humorous books and essays and take a shot at writing your own. Try to remember to look at life one day at a time instead of as a burden you'll be carrying for a long long time. Take stock in hope, because hope is a valuable commodity and it can't be traded or substituted.

Bereavement

When we lose someone we love, we need a forum to acknowledge, process, and resolve our grief. Bereavement, the loss of a significant someone to death, travel, divorce, or separation, can be a tremendously complex and severe psychological trauma. Perhaps the attachment you had to that person was exemplified in the feelings of security and completion they brought out in you. The loneliness you feel after they are gone is then one of emotional isolation, a separateness or an inability to connect. To an outsider these emotions can look like mood swings, anger, restlessness, and a turning inward. Denial often gives way to despair.

Dialogue. Although all bereavements are painful, the death of a loved one has some unique features. The bereaved may see the departed in a dream, or actually believe he has passed her in the street, until the permanence of the loss sets in.

Writing a dialogue, or imaginary conversation, with the deceased person can help you come to terms with the finality of the situation, the closing. Through this process you can gradually begin to let go of the person's life and its effect on yours, and at last to say *goodbye.* As you converse with the one who is gone, you can also clear your mind of what's nagging at you, what's left undone. Often the death of someone you love makes the mortality of your own life loom large. You can work on your feelings by writing about them.

Turn outward. If you use your journal to dream up and develop a definite goal, something altruistic to strive for, that will be a powerfully positive force for you. Muster the inner strength to establish some kind of community of friends or to meet people who have similar interests in work, religion, or politics. You may just find that they look after their members unselfishly. With time, you can reciprocate.

Here again are the *Venting, Realizing, and Coping Tools* in this chapter, and for your convenience, the page numbers on which they're explained:

Candle Concentration, page 57
Do Something Different, page 58
Unsent Letters, page 59
Stare It in the Face, page 59
Key Words, page 60
Reprioritize, page 60
Look at Expectations, page 61
Do a Word Portrait, page 61
Make Lists, page 61
What Holds You Back? page 61
Be Realistic, page 62
Time Reference, page 62
Stories, page 62
Banish Childhood Labels, page 63
Diffuse Hostility, page 64
Master Anger, page 64
Fight Back, page 66
Squaring Up, page 66
Self-Portrait, page 66
Make a Declaration, page 68
A Time to Look Within, page 68
Treating the Pain, page 69
Coping, page 69
Dialogue, page 70

Creative Action Checklist

❖ Put up a home bulletin board for family notices, household lists, and communication.

❖ Participate in an activity separately with each child. Make it a special outing or something the child suggests.

❖ If you are upset, don't force a showdown on things that don't really matter, like hair style, makeup, bedmaking, etc.

❖ Turn your family on to something new, like Chinese food one night instead of pizza, a foreign film, or attending a lecture together.

❖ Say "No" this week to a responsibility you really do not want.

Creative Comfort Checklist

❖ Make a list of your scariest and most positive thoughts about a project you are currently engaged in. Get your mate to exchange lists.

❖ Write an outrageous horoscope for all the people you will see tomorrow. Give each one a copy. "Planetary activity this month is . . ."

❖ Find out what your name looks like in Egyptian hieroglyphs. Practice learning how to write it.

❖ If you are feeling stressed, plan the simplest of meals. Heat up a hearty soup or soup combination, pick up a deli or fast-food salad, or make a supper of thick, chewy bread.

Chapter 5
Calendar

"Eight hours a night = four months a year of sleep."

— JEAN-LOUIS SERVAN-SCHREIBER
Examples of Durations

Where did the day go? Where did the year go? It's a fact of our sped-up modern lives that keeping track of time presents a real challenge. Our impatience with time exerts an ever-more-pervasive influence on who we are, as the thirty-minute sit-com and thirty-second sound bite increasingly control our expectations—to say nothing of our attention spans.

Technology contributes to this phenomenon. If the computer is a few seconds slow, it has the technician grumbling irritably. Think about that! In *The Art of Time*, Jean-Louis Servan-Schreiber tells a story about some passengers on an Air France Concorde aircraft. Apparently, on their arrival in New York, an electrical failure caused the exit door to bond shut. After seven minutes of this unforeseen delay, the passengers were putting together their demands for indemnities. After a fifteen-minute interval, with still no exit available, Servan-Schreiber says the passengers were agitated to the point of rioting.

Along with this chafing relationship people have with time goes a high degree of superficiality. We *do*, we *act*, but we don't *reflect*. As Servan-Schreiber says, "The skittish approach of modern times leads to doing nothing thoroughly, just so we can do more of it."

Plan to Plan

In your journal, the first step to rectifying this poor relationship with time is to figure out not "how much" or "how," but "why." This is really a way of keeping in touch with yourself. You should make a conscious daily effort to justify in writing the way you spend your precious time.

Do you know how time fits into your own life? Make a list and label it *Myself and Time.* Add up the hours that an average day provides for your usual tasks, including work, comfort, and the necessities. This is the beginning of helping you figure out what you want. Only you are aware of your own lapses with time—what makes you drift away from your purpose and what your unique failings and weaknesses are. To set a goal or plan, it makes sense that you need to know what you want first, and then factor in everything else that's unique to you.

To expand on this goal-planning exercise, the next step is careful observing. Subject your day to close scrutiny, trying to account for every minute. Write down what you have learned and call this blueprint *Time Designs.*

Now look at where the *clutter* is in your life. You are probably overloaded by outside influences without even being aware of it. Telephone calls, letters, interruptions: all these eat up our time. What are your clutters?

Henry David Thoreau recounts that once while taking his daily walk he came upon a glorious rock. The rock wooed him into thinking that it was something he had to possess. After much effort spent hauling it home, he displayed it proudly in his house, only to discover, after a time, that his rock showed dust. Dusting, he determined, was a major waste of time, and he hauled that rock back to its original place, where he could pass it by and enjoy it every day without any care on his part.

Above all, *Reflect.* This is the key to mastering your time. Set aside some time to think about where your hours go, and whether they are used to realize your goals.

When You're Unemployed

Being out of work hurts. It's hard on survival, it's hard on self-esteem, and it's hard on dignity. If this is happening to you, keep in mind that everyone faces challenges and problems, and that your ability to handle problems is important to your well-being and independence. What can you do in your journal to find a new beginning—a new job, a different career, an unfamiliar goal?

Rehearse

A good example of rehearsing is the story of Michael Bilich, general manager of F.A. Hoyt Ltd., a company that leases garbage collection equipment. The story is told by authors Michael Ray and Rochelle Myers in their book *Creativity in Business*. It seems that Bilich had once been one of the youngest vice-presidents in the history of Crocker Bank. He reached a plateau at work when he realized that to make any further contributions he would have to make sacrifices in other areas of his life. At that point, he says, he left, then immediately got into a panic thinking about how he should be working. He started looking for a job with that *should* bearing down on him. He couldn't find anything. Then, Bilich recalls, he got down on himself and worried frantically about what he was going to do and how he was going to make mortgage payments. After realizing that they could get by on his wife's income for a while, he went into what he calls his "monastic period."

Bilich said he would meditate, run for fitness, and read. He read over fifty books, books about history, philosophy, religion, and biology, during this period of unemployment. As his meditation skills improved, he began visualizing—*rehearsing* the kind of job he would want if he had the choice of doing anything in the world. He envisioned working in a small company owned by a wealthy person. In addition to managing the business, Bilich thought he would also like to manage the owner's money. Through a series of what seemed to be coincidences, he landed just that kind of job with F.A. Hoyt. There, using the same rehearsal techniques he had learned while meditating, he was able to triple the pretax earnings of the company in his first four years of employment.

By *rehearsing* you can find what it is that you are good at, what you have an aptitude for. This is more important to your business life than trying to alter your attitude. Armed with specific goals, you will bring a great enthusiasm to your work, and the sense that you are doing the job you are best fitted for.

As a teenager, Anaïs Nin wrote in her diary, "I fell asleep last night dreaming that I had taken [a short story] to a publisher who frightened me terribly and told me that I could do better. And now today, obsessed by that dream, I wrote another one that is much better."

Time Line

The time line is a simple yet illuminating exercise in planning and goal setting. With a ruler, and on a new page turned horizontally, draw a horizontal line through the center. This represents your life, from birth to about age 80. Your comments about "time past" will go above the line, and your "future plan" notes below.

Put a zero at the far left of the line and mark it with a vertical marker line. Put another marker at 80, on the far right. If you anticipate a longer and fuller life, by all means make that number as high as you wish. Set markers at regular intervals on your line so you can see, at a glance, your life at ages five, ten, fifteen, twenty, and so on, keeping in mind that five-year increments are just an easy notch of measure. Now think about these questions and write the answers above the line, over the corresponding years.

What have you done? What experiences have been valuable to you and when did they occur? What were the milestones in your life—you might include learning to walk, an event in elementary school, a religious confirmation, whatever was important to you then on up to the present. Think about what it is you've always had a passion for. What did you think about when you were alone in these younger lives you've lived? Who was part of your life then?

With the past and its reflections firmly and honestly planted in your mind, turn to the present. Ask yourself, What do I worry about? Who is influential in my life? Have I realized a passion from the past? What have I mastered? What kinds of advice do friends ask me for? What do I always wish I had more time for? If I could lead the life of an adventurer of grand proportions, how would I spend my time?

Having answered these questions, the next question is whether your answers will alter your time line when you start inserting your plans for the future. What do you want to accomplish, looking at the balance of time left on the life line? Have important feelings and desires been neglected? If someone told you you only have six months to live, would it make you feel more urgent about what you write on your life line? (This certainly gives new meaning to the expression, *putting your life on the line!*)

Now that you have a guide, look at it every six months or so to reinforce your newfound sense of direction and to keep current about what you want to establish for yourself. Give yourself positive rewards for remembering new directions or accomplishing a goal. In fact, set up a reward system now, while you are thinking about the total picture.

You know, a writer has no trouble with the beginning of a book. Ideas spill out onto the page almost faster than he or she can write them down, pouring out of the bubbling creative mind. The ending, too is usually known ahead of time. But ah, dear writer— the middle will drive you insane. Whether you are crafting fiction or your own life's time line, the muddling middle—what you need to do for the now—there's the rub.

Keeping a Family

After working on your personal time line is often the best time to look at your relationships with your children.

"Self-esteem," and its role in the life of the child, was the watchword for over a decade. The old seat-of-the-pants approach to parenting based on control and discipline gave way to its opposite, permissiveness. Parents forgot, for a time, how to say "No." This was the era of the baby boomer.

In time, the demands of propriety brought back a kind of balance. We see now that guidelines for conduct, behavior, and respect are not acquired willy-nilly. They are grounded in a personal philosophy and a well-thought-out plan. In your journal, devote some space to your relationship with your own children. Ask yourself questions and let your children, their behaviors, and their responses supply the answers. For example, What do I think is important for my children to learn? What traits and characteristics do I believe are valuable? If I could endow my child with any one quality, what would it be? What does he or she know of honesty and difficult choices?

You might want to conduct a *family survey* with your children. Ask them questions like, Who are your heroes? What do you think of revenge? What do you think morals and ethics are? Can you give examples of each? Is TV bad? What do you think of the violence in such-and-such a movie?

A writer friend of mine became concerned when, out of necessity, her work spilled over onto the family's dining area. She had to resign herself to the fact that her family would temporarily have to eat on TV trays in front of the television set. Since the family meals took place in early evening, they watched the PBS evening news and commentary, and before long she realized that her fears about her children becoming zombies in front of the television were unfounded. This family viewing time actually became the starting point for a new understanding with her children. She learned what their perceptions on current culture were, how they felt about issues such as congressional misconduct, abortion, drug wars, the prison system, racial disharmony, and world conflict. The writer might never have been able to broach such subjects with her children without this opportunity.

An excellent book to use in conjuction with your journal is *The Book of Questions*, by Gregory Stock. In it are an abundance of questions about concepts and beliefs. Some of the questions require a great deal of thought, because they are about moral dilemmas or making painful choices. You might think of buying a *family journal* and working through the book together, citing individual reactions and responses, and the date. What a fabulous vehicle this would be for rereading and reflection. What could be better than knowing how individuals in a family felt about the important things—along with the standard photographs and mementos?

Reflect

Reflection, as we have seen, is taking time to examine your life: to distinguish the essential from the merely important, to gain perspective on things that have happened, to identify needs, point out weaknesses, remind you of promises not yet fulfilled. But reflection has another meaning, too: it's the image that we see gazing back at us when we comb our hair, brush our teeth, pose in a vogue kind of way—straight on. What the mirror cannot show us is the way we look when we chew, how our mouth moves when we talk, our distinctive walk, the way our hands fidget with our clothes when we discuss money matters, etc. A *video tape* of yourself going about your ordinary activities could be a revelation. Why don't you take turns with a trusted friend following the other around for a few hours and filming? Watch the results when you are alone, and write about what you learned and felt.

Expose yourself to the sound of your own speech by making an audiotape. Are the tones your voice returns to your ears too high, grating, or unclear? You would be surprised how much there is to learn from this simple exercise. Make your journal notes the basis for future action and growth.

Write Your Horoscope

People love to read the psychic forecasts about what their week, month, or year will be like. It's a safe way to "predict" your future, and if your horoscope is in alignment with what you want for yourself, you will be pleased as well as entertained.

Why not use your inner guide to craft your own horoscope? You can make predictions about your work life and success, write about your prospects for a new love life, and pick on which calendar days you want fortune to smile handsomely on you. You can even plot your own moon's rising (body cycles) and anticipate what effect it will have on your skin, your feelings, and your luck.

Why do you think astrological forecasting appears under the chapter about goals and planning, instead of creative thinking? Because the power of imagining the best for yourself and picking definite days for those wonderful things to come about can affect the way things happen to you, and that is more closely wedded to positive planning than creative dreaming. Your intuition and attitude about the future can set up a flow toward your mission or purpose. It's true. The more compassion you have for yourself, and the better your attitude is when you write your horoscope, the more likely you will be to nurture your abilities—and to reach your dream or goal.

You can also write (in horoscope language) as if your goal had already been reached. Athletes are trained physically and mentally to do this all the time. The runner pictures herself cutting through the finish line tape before it happens; the golfer pictures that perfect follow-through just before he addresses the tee; the swimmer is reaching fingertips for the wall before she gets there. The visualization becomes a self-fulfilling prophecy, and it can work for you too.

After you write your predictions, you might look them over to see what they reveal. Have you written about the essentials? Is there pessimism for the future, or have you been positive and hopeful? If you were screenwriting or scripting your future, what would it look like? The future lies within you: seize it!

Creative Action Checklist

❖ Picture and draw your life in the shape of a goal pyramid. What is at the bottom and what do you expect at the top? Be realistic, but not overly realistic or you might set your expectations too low. Plan a series of rewards for reaching the different plateaus.

❖ Visualize your life five or ten years ahead. Focus on what you're doing, eating, and wearing, where you're working, who you are loving, what you are dreaming.

❖ Do at least one thing to create a new environment for yourself. This could mean buying a painting, moving furniture, or making a rug.

❖ In your journal, write an essay à la Andy Rooney about a favorite pet peeve of yours.

Creative Comfort Checklist

❖ Write a mini-biography of what you have accomplished in your life to date.

❖ Listen to a humorous audio tape—all the way through without distraction.

❖ Buy yourself that golf video you've been wanting.

❖ Take inventory of your beliefs. What philosophy could you impart to others from your own career or life choices?

Chapter 6

Connections

"Men can starve from a lack of self-realization
as much as they can from a lack of bread."
— RICHARD WRIGHT, *Native Son*

Looking back on your childhood can do several things, but the first reason to do it is that it satisfies a genuine need. Thinking about the past gives you the ability to touch the naive child you once were, in a less complicated time. By traveling back, you realize how far you have come. Sometimes this process is like gathering up and reshuffling life's cards; it puts your life into a new context so you are remixed (not a "stacked deck") and ready for the game—the game of now.

The second and perhaps more valuable reason for childhood reflection is that reconnecting with the past gives insight into the *behavior patterns* you have developed over your lifetime. Such patterns can become a template for the way you react to everything in your life today. To carry the analogy further, seeing your childhood as a template fashioned from your parents' influence and your earlier life experiences can provide insight into some of the puzzling feelings we have today.

The problems that are troubling you, indeed, may result from such ingrained behaviors. You are using the same pattern on everything you do, perhaps, but trying to create different products. The answer is not to put blame on your parents or your surroundings but to realize and embrace the fact that, barring child abuse, your parents raised you the best they knew how. All parents make mistakes. If you are a parent yourself, it may be comforting to remember that no one, no matter who his or her parents, can be brought up without any future pain or problems. All of us need to come to grips with old habits and patterns, shed the blame, and develop new ways to tackle things.

The purpose of writing about your childhood is not to dredge up painful feelings. If you have problems as a result of verbal, physical, or sexual abuse in childhood, that should be worked out with a sensitive therapist. It is not realistic to expect your journal to absorb and direct all that anger and pain. Seek outside help for abuse problems.

Some of the best ways to recover lost feelings and memories are through *photographs, key words, visualization,* and *sensory stimulus.* Smelling something with a familiar or exotic essence can bring memories up, as can the touch of an old velvet dress or the soft ears of your family's cocker spaniel. Hearing an old song is a great way to jog your brain, whether it is the strains of a commercial's jingle or the first song you slow-danced to.

Take some time to build a *memory box.* In it you will collect the objects that will help you touch the past. Find and organize baby pictures; class pictures; milestone photos of your first step, your first pony ride, your swimming lessons, your confirmation or bar mitzvah, your first car, your prom date, your graduation, and your marriage. Add to this any early school papers and drawings. Did your mother save childhood sketches, cartoons, or musings? Collect in your memory box any awards you earned, badges, or other markers of your academic, religious, or personal education.

Ask your parents whether you can retrieve any old toys from your past. These are perhaps one of the best amulets for recalling left-behind days; the toys you carried, manipulated, and imagined with. Since play is a major portion of a child's life, that may be a good starting place for reconstructing your childhood in your journal. Write down what occupied your free hours. Who was there? Can you recall your favorite books? Was jump rope popular in your neighborhood? The hula hoop? Hopscotch? Can you recall the acrid smell of your first cap gun, or the trigger action of an air rifle? Do you have photos of a Christmas gift granted from your "wish list"?

Try to recapture that playful mood you had when you were lit-tler. Even play injuries you carry today can help spark a play mem-ory: a chipped tooth from falling during a skipping game, a slight gash over your eye from standing too close to a batter, an elbow scar from playing S-P-U-D on the brick streets in your neighborhood—these can be valuable memory aids. Moreover, think about it: after the crying and the bandage, what happened? Life went on. You sur-vived. You might even have learned something. Did you overcome your fear of doctors? Did that broken arm teach you that you could indeed heal and overcome a problem quickly?

Write about what it was like to be on a team—do you remem-ber any of your teammates? What is it like to think of yourself as part of a group, as playing a sport for a community effort? The black eye, the bruise on the chest, the skinned knee—were they bodily sacri-fices for the team—you gotta expect it—or was it more the pride of being able to "take it"?

Remember the pride of your first swimming pool dive, or learning how to keep that two-wheeler up all by yourself. Did you have a treehouse, or a clubhouse? Secret initiations or blood oaths with your friends? What was the code of conduct for fairness in play? Were you always cast as Blackie the Bad Guy in gun fights? What kinds of missions did you imagine for your green army men? Did you invite Teddy to lunch and bake cookies on your Betty Crocker electric stove?

Was it important in play to emulate your mother's role, and did she encourage quieter efforts in play? Did your father solicit you to help with the "manly stuff" around the house? All of these feel-ings can help define who you are today, and why.

If you are finding it hard to remember, call up a favorite aunt, a neighborhood friend, or an old school chum. With a pot of coffee and some old photographs or mementos, it probably won't be long before you are sharing and remembering flashes of days gone by.

Sometimes, returning to a childhood scene, either in person or in your mind, can help zero in on memories. Be cautioned, though, that a return trip to one's childhood home, school yard, or church can often create more depression than nostalgia. One often hears about someone revisiting his or her old haunts and becoming outraged at what the current owners have done, or depressed because what they remembered was much larger, less worn. Of course things looked bigger then: you've grown. And often nostalgia makes the places of our youth seem grander, less hard-edged.

Close your eyes and think about where it was you ate your meals. It might help you to recall your favorite foods: a child will often go through a period of eating nothing but peanut butter and bananas or macaroni and cheese. Okay, go with that. Where did you sit when you spread your peanut butter? Do you remember having to climb up onto a stool to reach the counter? Can you see the kitchen clock? One journal writer vividly remembers a Kit Kat clock and the way the eyes moved back and forth with the pendulum tail. He also remembers how the clock lulled him into sleep one day while he waited to return to school after lunch, and how the tears poured down his cheeks as he ran breathlessly up the hill to catch the school bus. To this day he is always punctual. These are *unconscious lessons.*

The past helps shape what is active in the present. Maybe you wonder why you have had trouble giving up a certain habit. By walking with this action back through the past, you can find out how it came about, and in this way, perhaps loosen the behavior's hold on you. It could work. Of course, try to keep in mind that reliving scenes from the past should be a positive thing. It is not meant to torment you or change your version of the world, but to strengthen and teach you.

What about your play? How did the way you played affect the person you grew up to be? You might ask yourself, for instance, whether it had any relation to the way you now approach employment, responsibilities, and coworkers. Leave the scenes of your home for a while and think about your outside world, the world of playgrounds, neighborhood, and games. Think about your typical summer day. You've just eaten a bowl of your favorite breakfast cereal when through the screen door you hear the familiar sing-song strain of a neighborhood friend calling you out to play. Where do you meet the guys? Do you head over to the playground? Climb up to a treehouse? Swing a leg over your bike? Grab the skates in the garage?

Take a look inside your jeans pocket. What do you find? Maybe it's really hot and you've got a new water gun. You split a grape popsicle with your sister; later, your mom will turn on the sprinkler. Or maybe today is the day you set up your Kool-Aid stand, 10¢ a glass.

Were there recurring themes in your play—games of deciding power, becoming leader of the posse, or engaging in espionage? Maybe you enjoyed the role of teacher—or maybe you felt out of place, an outcast. Perhaps you didn't join a group but stuck with that one special friend. How has your childhood role stayed with you, influencing your adult self?

Look back and try to get a picture of your parents. Anaïs Nin wrote in her diary as a teenager, "My disposition is a faithful copy of Papa's. With one single difference: his is noble in its weakness and wonderful even with all his faults, while mine is like that of a child who has been badly brought up because of a change of teachers . . ."

Do you recognize the relationship your father had with your mother, and has it had an effect on what you've wanted in your own relationships, loves, and marriage? What was their attitude toward money? Did they entertain or play cards? What kinds of people were they? How different were your parents from each other, and did they share some values? Where do you fit into this scenario? When did you first feel like your own person? What were you trying to become?

In a book entitled *Here At The New Yorker*, writer Brendan Gill observes, "One spends a lifetime reconstructing one's past, and it is not merely in order to find an image of oneself that will prove pleasing; rather, it is in order to approach some tentative, usable truth about oneself by ransacking all the data that have hovered dimly somewhere 'out there,' helping to form one's nature. If the unexamined life is not worth living, the unexamined past is not worth possessing; it bears fruit only by being held continuously up to the light, and it is as changeable and as full of surprises, pleasant and unpleasant, as the future."

Portraits of Influential People

All your life your relationships are based on identifying with others. You take in information from those around you and identify selectively with them, consciously or unconsciously deciding what you will accept for yourself. You say, *I am organized, like my mother; stubborn, like my dad.* Your image of yourself is a unique composite of everyone who has had an influence on you.

It is interesting and important to write a word portrait of the important people in your life. After you have described what makes them distinctive in your eyes, make a list of the qualities and characteristics you've taken for yourself. Judith Viorst, author of *Necessary Losses*, says, "We identify for many reasons and usually for several reasons at once. And we often identify to deal with loss, preserving within oneself—by acquiring, say, the style of dress, the accent, the mannerisms—of someone we must leave or someone who dies."

After completing this exercise, you might want to look at your own identity. Look at such things as sense of humor and tone of voice, and the way you use flattery on others to ease a tense situation. Look thoroughly at the *legacy of behavior* you leave, and would choose to leave, for your own heirs and those who are under your influence.

For those with chronic feelings of sadness or low self-esteem, an interesting experiment has come by way of clinical psychologist Penelope Russianoff, Ph.D., author of *When Am I Going to Be Happy?* She suggests that you go back and take care of the "inner child," see yourself as someone worthy of affection. She believes that if, as a child, you didn't feel valued and cared for, as an adult you will carry that image along with you. She suggests you find your most hated photo of yourself as a child and have it blown up to poster size. Hang it on your closet door, and every day look at it and ask yourself, *If I were that little girl's mother, how could I make her feel loved?* Your follow up is to imagine taking that earlier you into your waiting arms, cuddling her and lavishing on her all the strokes and love you can give.

Write down what you will do for your inner child, what you might do to stick up for that kid—acting as if you were standing up for a best friend besieged by a rival group. By listening to the child you once were, you can use this befriending tactic to bring courage to who you are today.

Creative Action Checklist

❖ This week at least, keep your home life and your job separate. If your work life is well organized, leave it behind when you walk out the door.

❖ Tell yourself to really listen to everyone tomorrow. It takes work.

❖ Demonstrate the power of a gift in one of your relationships.

❖ If your family life is mundane, think about getting a foreign exchange student. But understand the commitment and the responsibility and expect change.

Creative Comfort Checklist

❖ Write down what was a good time for you. What happened exactly?

❖ Who do you miss? If possible, give that person a call and say you miss him or her.

❖ Have your parents tell you a good family story. Tape it or put it on video.

❖ If you're sick of crowds or bogged down in the city, find out when the grocery store, mall, gas station, exercise facility, or favorite vacation spot is the least crowded, and go then. Or find those same services in a rural area on a planned Saturday.

.

Chapter 7

Insights

"I saw a muskrat come out of a hole in the
ice . . . While I am looking at him, I am thinking what he is thinking of me. He is a different sort of man, that is all."

— HENRY D. THOREAU , *Journal*

When we see someone holding a camera, we usually assume that
person is about to photograph another person or subject in order
to capture that moment on film. So when we see the photographer
turn the camera on himself and snap his own photo, that strikes us
as funny. The man behind the camera has turned the tables on
what is expected, surprising us by saving his own image for posterity.

In this chapter, you will, in essence, be turning the camera on
yourself—asking important questions, looking at recurrent self
problems, and developing your own philosophy.

Doodle

Doodling is an easy way to begin this process. It puts you into
a less constrained state of mind. The old adage the "brain knows it,
the hand shows it" is based on what people have put on paper in
their different dispositions. For example, if you are feeling straightforward, you may demonstrate that by drawing arrows (figure 1).
On the other hand, someone who feels secretive or withdrawn will
make small, tight, closed-off circles (figure 2). Steps would indicate

that someone feels ambitious, ready to climb the heights and take on a higher level (figure 3). A resentful or angry mood seems to be shown in a drawing with sharp points or angles (figure 4).

Just as the pyramid symbol was the sign of strength and showed the conquest of nature for the pharaohs, the drawing of a pyramid is the doodle of a powerful, strong-willed mind (figure 5), while for a state of introspection, our minds will take on a relaxed and easy-going state if we fill the paper with easy, loopy strokes or relaxed, ever-growing circles (figure 6). Try it.

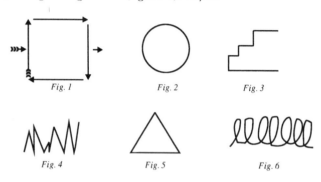

Fig. 1   Fig. 2   Fig. 3

Fig. 4   Fig. 5   Fig. 6

You may put your doodles in the margins of your paper or use them as letterhead or footnotes. If you're tense, use your relaxed hand symbols to fill up an entire page before you go on to the other examples.

Tracking Emotions

Try using simple graphs to chart your emotions. Nothing elaborate; all you'll be doing is approximating your feelings by the position of dots on the paper, using the accumulated data to compare your mental well-being with your physical health. For example, you may feel your emotional state to be frazzled, angry, and full of impatience today. Put a dot on the lower third of the paper, over on the left-hand side. The lower third of the paper supposes you're in the dumps. The middle section could be average or normal feelings. The upper section would be reserved for elevated moods. Alongside the dot, put a mood statement; write out your mental self-talk. If the feeling is exhaustion, perhaps you are thinking that you were off-center today because your paperwork is undone, or you're angry because dinner will have to be take-out and you're stuck picking it up. Write it down.

Now turn the page and, in the lower third of the paper again, just about the same area as your first dot, write down what your body is telling you about being frazzled. Do you have a headache? Is your vision fuzzy or your eyes heavy? Are your shoulders curved in, your midriff squashed? Maybe you feel itchy, or your feet seem swollen. By charting your emotions next to your thoughts, then graphing your own physical state, you can begin to see unique physiological connections.

At first you may not be able to do much about the way you feel when you are in the lower third of the page. With time, though, and the increased awareness that your physical well-being is closely linked with your state of mind, you can take steps to draw yourself up higher.

Alarm Clock Exercise

This plan calls for some advance setup and the cooperation of another person, but the results should be spontaneous. Buy an alarm watch and have a friend privately set the alarm to go off at random intervals during the day—you will have no idea of when. When you hear the alarm, immediately write down what you are thinking and how you feel at that instant. The name of this technique is *tracking*, and it is used to show you the range of your moods in the course of just one day.

Metaphors

A metaphor, according to *Webster's New World Dictionary*, is a figure of speech in which one thing is spoken of as if it were another. Try to give metaphors your own personal twist. For example, the phrase "on cloud nine" will become, "I am on cloud nine." "Today Madeline felt tickled pink," and so on. Metaphors can give new names to things and renew your language. Collect these vivid and daring figures of speech from friends or readings. Create new ones and give them your own personal pronoun. Set aside a page for them. Turn down the corner for quick access and check them when you need a shot of confidence or a kind of self-affirmation.

How-To Power

In the play *Auntie Mame*, Mr. Babcock, a trustee for eleven-year-old Patrick Dennis, has come to advise Miss Dennis on the rearing of her nephew. When he arrives, Patrick invites him in and makes him a martini. Babcock gets flustered when he is caught drinking during business hours, and defends himself by asking Mame Dennis how an innocent child knew how to concoct such a drink. Her retort is short and sweet: "Knowledge is power."

Your knowledge and your know-how have been *your* power. Have you forgotten how much you know? In an essay called, "Don't Just Sit There: Writing as a Polymorphous Perverse Pleasure," Rosellen Brown suggests that one make a list of all the things one knows. ". . . how to make fudge, how to give the Heimlich maneuver, how to get from New York to Miami on five dollars." (Now that's something we'd all like to know!) She calls this exercise her plan for stopgap ideas when nothing important will come in writing.

Can you imagine all that you, yourself, have managed to learn and master over the course of a lifetime? Take stock; rank your skills in order of competence and enjoyment. It's an awesome list. Your catalog will be just the thing to illustrate your accomplishments. Check it to get a new perspective when you are feeling useless or believe you have missed out on something.

Priority Review

How well do your ideals match your actions? Perhaps you say that money is not as important as your family—yet you are reluctant to take even the smallest percentage of the weekend off for a family event without the fax, the phone, or the notebook? Or you may be dieting or shopping extensively to conform to a model's image or to get the approving look of strangers—yet telling yourself that you are not concerned with superficialities, that your affection is meant for those closest to you? You say you believe in respect for all people, and yet it is not enough for you to win at something—an account, a business deal or a major company decision: you are so competitively aggressive that someone else has to lose, too.

Maybe it's time to examine mixed messages. Write down your current beliefs and principles, the things you declare about yourself to others. Then, in another column, grade how important these current ideas really are to you. 1–Of utmost importance, 2–Very important, 3–Somewhat important, 4–Somewhat unimportant. Now you can ask, is it what you really mean? Is the goal or desire still worth what you need to get it? Keep it? What we tell others through actions, compared to what we would like to believe, is crucial to self-respect and to our relationships with others.

You and Others

This is a powerful exercise to try if your relationships are feeling colder, more distant. Make two lists. In the first column you will write, under the heading *I and Them*, how you treated the members of your family, immediate circle, or community at various points in the day. Where and when did you interact with them, and how did it go? For example, you may remember, thinking back, that your daughter deposited bank drafts for you, and that you only cursorily acknowledged her gesture, dismissing it with a wave or a nod of the head. Write this down. Now, in the *New Awareness* column, write down what the other person's needs might be, being aware of their actions, feelings, and motives. In this case, your daughter spent time doing your task; why? To save you time? To get a payback? Out of respect? What about your response—can you alter it next time? Will the outcome be different? It is sometimes hard to remember to give affirmations, and yet they are so important to the growth of a relationship.

Sexuality

The journal is a wonderfully private place to explore and define what sensuality and sexuality mean to you. For some, sensuality refers to a physical response and sexuality a mental one: sexuality then is a matter of intending an erotic experience. Diarist Christina Baldwin claims that she, at least, has not been able to remove the vocabulary boundaries that are set to define and delineate sensuality and sexuality. In her book *One to One*, she writes about sensual awareness as "the natural extension of feelings . . . limited only by our inhibitions."

We all possess an invisible boundary around ourselves. This phenomenon is commonly referred to as the "psychic circle," or "bubble." It is an area of privacy that extends about two feet beyond our bodies; if anyone comes closer than that two feet, we feel un-comfortable. Ask yourself whether you have been aware of this feel-ing. Do you sometimes avoid breaking your bubble of privacy by reaching out to others, without knowing why or what holds you back? Many studies have shown that even in fetuses, touch is the first sense to develop, and in newborns it is an automatic response even be-fore a baby begins to make sense of the world. Knowing that, why are you keeping yourself from being touched, hugged, caressed?

Recording your desires and sexual needs in your journal is a healthy approach to answering such questions, and a good way to be aware of the subtle details of nonverbal communication between yourself and those who enter your inviolate space.

Tristine Rainer, author of *The New Diary*, says that erotic writing in diaries seems to fall into five categories: sexual memories, com-plaints, celebrated experiences, erotic dreams and fantasies, and be-havioral rehearsals for sexual encounters.

Sensual History

Write about your sexual history. What were some of the first sensations that made you aware of your body? Do you remember the first time you felt curious enough to explore those tendencies? Did you fantasize romantically and/or sexually about television or movie stars? Do you remember your perceptions changing and your desires directed more toward your dreams or ideals? What did you assume your married life or romantic relationships would be like? How do you feel about your own body? Have you denied your true feelings and even faked an orgasm or pretended to be content? What led to that experience? Do you want to change anything about your private life?

Change Your Point of View

Often writers are so uncomfortable trying to articulate their desires that in order to find a way to communicate with their sexual selves, they use a change of persona, using "he" or "my friend" to write in a dialogue. If you are uncomfortable but want to ask your inner self questions, the new persona may help you bridge cultural inhibitions. It can be a surprisingly effective way to unearth our in-terrelated emotional needs.

Changing your point of view can help you to discover episodes of longing in your sexual history—and perhaps clarify what you don't want. For example: *Sensual you: why do you kill your own needs by acting cold or inhibited?*

I don't want a passive sexual role in this relationship and I do not want to mask over my urges, so why do I pretend to speak a passive language of love with phoney slang or clinical phrases? I hate that. I've got to be more open and say what I want to in my own words, my own talk. Maybe this sex talk feels unnatural or scripted, like a part I'm playing, and is too immature for the way I'm really feeling.

This point-to-point dialogue with your libido can help you begin to observe the sensuality you feel about yourself in relation to others.

Ode to Your Body

In another context, try to examine any anxieties you may feel about your own body. Craft a positive *love story or poem* about your physical features, combating the urge to measure them against some Hollywood standard of perfection. Dedicate your ode to the beauties of generous thighs, small genitals or breasts, or absent or abundant hair. Forgive and compliment your limbs, whether bony or soft, and work your prose up to include your warm, soft hands, your tender, pouting lips, and the mystery of your personal smell. Set your creative energy loose with free verse.

Hidden Feelings

In his book *When All You've Ever Wanted Isn't Enough,* Rabbi Harold Kushner explains that we are often at war with ourselves. We love food but we agonize over our diets, we crave sexual pleasure and then ponder over whether it is pleasure we want or shameful self-indulgence. Feelings of hate and scorn threaten our peace and contentment. Lots of mixed messages. Kushner says, "We are afraid of never having lived, of coming to the end of our days with the sense that we were never really alive, that we never figured out what life was for."

Unsent Letter

A good journal technique for figuring out the *I don't know what's wrong, but I don't feel happy* phase, is to write an *unsent* letter to yourself. In it, talk about what gives you pleasure. Try to be specific with your descriptions, using concrete images such as, Being able to figure out the end to mystery novels early on . . . The hint of cologne that's left on her clothes . . . The view of a mountain range off in the horizon from a good vantage point . . . and so on.

"100" Lists

Lisa Friedman, in an article for *New Woman* (December 1992) tells about a seminar she took. Her objective was to recapture the pleasure in her life. As part of the exercises assigned to the group, they were to make lists: "100 things that you are grateful for," "100 things you would like to do before dying," "100 things you can do to nurture yourself." The lists, she says, have a hidden lesson. "All of us begin writing enthusiastically, then get stuck around the thirtieth item. Pushing past number thirty helps your ideas flow—and opens new vistas for enjoyment."

Try these when you're looking for meaning, relaxation, and inspiration. Make up some "100" lists of your own.

Unstalling

A fun kind of psychological test conducted with symbols might be just the thing to try when you approach your journal with a need to write but are frustrated about where to begin.

There are seven symbols:

At the top of the page, put these symbols in an order of importance. You will not know what the icons are supposed to represent yet, but that does not matter. You are hoping to achieve a kind of stream of consciousness. Every few months or so, go back to the symbols and again rank them in order, in the hierarchy that is most pleasing to you. Check the key for the signs' meanings, and then write a dialogue with yourself about whether the particular order makes sense to you. You may be surprised to see how your unconscious choices show the reprioritizing you are continually doing throughout the year.

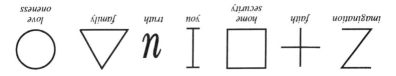

Family Journal

This is something that can be done with the other members of your family during the Christmas or Chanukah season. Keep a separate book or steno pad available and ask each person in the family to write a paragraph every day this month. Describe it as a kind of advent calendar or a countdown to the big day. Put different topic headings on the pages like, "What I'm Thankful For" or "How I Could Treat My Parents (or Kids) Better" and so on. You might let each person take turns making up that day's theme. The writing can take the form of a list, a drawing, or a poem, something that children can look forward to. A family tradition may emerge from this exercise, and it could also provide an opportunity for discussion.

Decision Help

Abraham A. Low, M.D. the founder of Recovery, Inc.—a group offering improved mental health through will training—believed that it was of utmost importance that people be able to make their own decisions.

Your journal is a wonderful place to practice independent decision making. Try following these steps.

1. Pick one thing to deal with at a time. By determining the most important, you can direct your energies and work through your list systematically.

2. Seek other input. If you gather as much information as you can, you will be able to formulate more knowledge-able opinions. Listen to those who don't agree with you. It is not unwise to change your opinion about things, but it is unwise not to consider other suggestions.

3. Weigh your options by knowing the pluses and minuses of all the plans.

4. Pay attention to what your intuition tells you.

5. Determine your choice.

6. Write it down and avoid the pressure of a forced answer or of trying to remember the issue for awhile. Sleep on it if possible.

7. If, in the end, the result was not what you wanted, accept the mistake as quickly as you can and try to correct it.

8. Log the outcome for future decision reference and confidence. You may not be right all the time, but you don't have to repeat your mistakes, either.

Mood Changers

Sometimes we would like to feel a different way. Perhaps we are tired or disgusted, or yes, just moody. You can use your journal to help minimize these feelings. Try the following steps; eventually, you may find yourself devising your own methods.

Fill a page with loops. When an artist is trying to loosen some tension before beginning a pencil sketch, he or she often makes large, loose scribbles on the page. Writing mirrors what you feel inside, and this pendulous movement helps you relax.

When you write, write all the way over to meet the right margin. Try not to curb in your script or avoid the full page but reach for it, moving into the future.

Write about your last good laugh. What struck you as so funny? Write about the changes that took place in your physical self. Did your hair get disheveled? Did you get carried away and make unusual sounds, or laugh until your sides ached? Maybe your eyes teared up and that made your glasses slip down and your nose run. How hilarious and awkward we are when we're really laughing! Can you picture it? Can you remember when you last laughed like that? Write down your memory of it.

Truth Check

James W. Pennebaker, who has invested many hours in journal

study programs with his students at Southern Methodist University, says to look for words of self-testimony. Pennebaker says that when the words *really, honestly,* or *truly* show up in an explanation, it usually indicates inhibition. Words of attestation used to back up a situation, such as when people absolutely *assure* you, or themselves, that they are telling the truth, generally occur before the writer has progressed to the stage of accepting a problem—and before they're ready to divulge it.

Go back and look for those words in your journal. Reexamine the context to see whether that is how you actually feel or felt about a situation. If not, write about how the subject has changed in your mind.

Fortify Your Will

What is willpower? These days it's often associated with eating. Can we avoid the sweet taste we crave, skip an entrée bathed in rich sauce, or give up a fat-based, nutritionless snack? Although the power to control diet choices could be defined as exercising willpower, our will is actually the basis of self-control for all attempts of change. It is the self-discipline, or *resolve,* that engineers the start and stop of everything we do.

Whatever it is you hope to accomplish—stopping a habit or compulsion, creating better health for yourself, or strengthening your commitment to produce a better product, relationship, or budget—your will is the energy to turn your vision into reality. In your journal, you can work to fortify your willpower, to pump up your resolve. Here are some steps you can use.

Ask yourself these questions. When was the last time you exerted your will for change? What did you accomplish? Did you have complications? How did you handle them? What could you say you learned from your change, and was it worth it?

1. *Practice.* List some things you can do to warm up your resolve. When you are at the office party, can you say "No, thank you" to an alcoholic beverage or a calorie-laden hors d'oeuvre and stick with that decision? Can you avoid engaging in rumor talk or disparaging conversation about another? Where can you exercise your will or won't power?

2. *Outline* some manageable steps. Try to break your goal down into smaller, more realistic steps. Rather than imagining that your task can be done in one sweep, it may be more sensible to look at the desired change as taking place over the long term.

3. *Reinforce* your ultimate goal. As you make some smaller positive changes, mark off each step you have taken with a highlighter. Write "Done" over each transition accomplished. This will serve as encouragement and enable you to see that, yes, things are happening in a planned way.

4. *Off-track?* Make a deal with yourself. Provide some kind of stimulus or reward for each step achieved. For example, you might give yourself a small gift or engage in a special activity if you manage to make a change.

5. *Deter temptation.* There will always be something waiting to sabotage your good intentions. Before temptation whispers in your ear, plan ahead by having a set of distractions ready. If your goal is to avoid overeating, your first distraction could be to take a brisk evening walk instead of watching food commercials on television and agonizing. Have another distraction technique ready in case you need it. Maybe you could put on headphones and listen to music next, or call a friend to chat.

   With an exceptionally strong desire or compulsion, you may even have third, fourth, or fifth alternate behaviors lined up. Write them all down in advance. Deepak Chopra, M.D., in his *Magical Mind, Magical Body* tape series, says that a variety of techniques are used successfully in drug clinics to diminish the withdrawal symptoms associated with drugs. Techniques include eating certain foods to balance specific body types, needs, and cravings; aromatherapy, the use of smells and essences; and assaulting the senses with new sights, sounds, and sensations, such as full-body massage with sesame oil. Write down and seek out your own best alternatives.

6. *Anticipate difficulties.* Write out a dialogue with yourself when you experience a failed attempt. In this talk with

your will, be ready to forgive a single failure and keep on keeping on. What is it you expected? Outline what you may face in pursuing your new goal or change. Say, for example, that you want to quit smoking. You can write to your expectations.

Expectations, what do I need to know in advance?
A. Expect people to comment on your bad temper. Expect to find the craving for a cigarette worse around the holidays or when you are under stress or are holding an alcoholic drink. Expect some opposition from your smoking friends. Expect to hear stories about how others have quit, and their suggestions, good or bad, for your individual needs.

What kinds of feelings will I experience?
A. Know that you may feel alone, even persecuted or paranoid at times. A change is very personal, and others will sometimes say discouraging, irritating, or stupid things. Expect that you may be afraid. Afraid of failing, afraid of being weak, afraid of asking for help. You may want to give up, even feel militant about giving up and getting others to join you.

How long will it take?
A. Considering how long you have smoked, you can expect the craving to last a while. You might want to take care of other current stresses first before undertaking this task. Give yourself time and space in which to accomplish it.

Will I ever be free of this habit?
A. You will most likely miss your old behavior, even find yourself dwelling fondly on your memories of "lighting up." Nostalgia for smoking will come when you are most vulnerable or stressed, or when you see others do it. Be prepared.

Why can't I be like my boss? She seems so strong, so assured of herself and her habits.
A. You are only human. Self-criticism is natural, and

you will most likely experience more of it as you work at a change. Maturity comes from recognizing this as temporary and knowing that new confidence will come as you practice and achieve each small step.

Develop Your Spirituality

Over time, in the course of your journal discovery, you may come to question your purpose, the meaning of your life, and even your own mortality.

Rabbi Harold Kushner tells the story of the Bible figure Ecclesiastes, the teacher. Ecclesiastes, he says, looked in vain for the meaning in life. Try as he would, he could never find it. "But despite his repeated failures, he could not bring himself to conclude that life was meaningless. He saw and felt futility, the injustice of so much that happens to us on earth. But at the same time, he sensed that life, however muddled and frustrating, was too sacred, too special, too full of possibilities to be meaningless . . . . At last, he found it not in a few great deeds but in thousands of little ones."

The journal is a good place to commune with yourself. To plot out what makes you feel you have purpose. To plan, question, and create your own personal deeds. You might copy favorite verses from your Bible or write out special prayers for yourself and others. Ask yourself, what is meant by your soul? Where do you feel most spiritually moved? What is your concept of Heaven?

A worldwide view of harmony is expressed in many religions, and the Golden Rule appears in Buddhism, Confucianism, Hinduism, Taoism, Islam, Judiasm, and Christianity. What is your essential spiritual message for yourself and others?

Creative Action Checklist

❖ Plan to watch the sky. Set your alarm for dawn and catch the sunrise, or visit a planetarium to look through a celestial telescope.

❖ Make a visit to look at your favorite painting, Van Gogh, Picasso, Renoir, or whatever. Go see the real thing, not a copy.

❖ Make your face up like a clown, or go to a place where you can have your picture taken in costume.

- Find a new passion. Little Rock, AR television news anchor Susan Rodman once covered bungee jumping news by doing it live—you can find your own passion too.
- Listen to New Age music, an opera performance, or rap—whatever you are not currently tuning in to.

Creative Comfort Checklist

- Order strawberries or orchids out of season.
- Go through old love letters, postcards, or albums.
- Invite a colleague of a different nationality or ethnic background to lunch.
- Learn how to use your new software program and teach someone else.
- Rotate your subscriptions to magazines and order a periodical that is not necessarily "you." For example, if you are an adult male, order *Teen* magazine for a season; a woman can subscribe to *Esquire*, an elderly citizen can take *Mad*.

Chapter 8

Questions and Answers

"The mind is its own place, and in itself
Can make a heaven of Hell, a hell of Heaven."
— JOHN MILTON , *Paradise Lost*

During the course of learning a new discipline, practicing a new technique, or adding to your sourcebook of knowledge, questions arise. Here are some of the more common questions that have come up about journal writing. They are compiled from inquiries that have come up at journal writing classes, informal discussions with friends and other writers, and in interviews with social workers, therapists, and educators.

Q: When I first sit down to write I have a horrible time getting started, and I feel frustrated. Is this normal for something I am so interested in?

A: This is not an uncommon reaction. For those who do not write in their daily work, it is not difficult to see how facing a blank page could be a source of frustration.

Before you start, find a place where you feel comfortable and secure, and somewhere where you will not be distracted. If your attention is divided by other, more pressing activities, get them out of the way first so that you will associate writing with something you do for yourself, not with something you have to do, like mopping the floor. Writing should be a pleasant experience.

Don't expect immediate results. By taking your time and allowing insights to develop, you will avoid the temptation to base your feelings on low-level intuitive thinking.

Maybe the best and most enjoyable way for you to get started would be to doodle or scrawl some large loopy designs. Another approach is to make a map of your past day's activity, or to cluster a word you would like to think about in more depth. Get started on any device that sounds interesting to you, and often the reticence that comes with approaching something new will disappear as you become absorbed in the process.

Q: Why write a goal down? I have goals in mind and I think about what I want. What would be the difference between my mental method and your journal writing plans?

A: Mental planning, visualizing, and mental rehearsal are all good thinking techniques. But in addition to these activities, it is extremely important to write your goals down.

Putting your objectives into writing reinforces them—and also helps you break them down into manageable segments. Are you looking at the short-term, mid-range, and long-term requirements of attaining your goal? By picturing and writing down where you want to be six months, one year, five years, or ten years down the road, you can better see the steps needed for realization. Dating your journal entries helps remind you where you thought you would be and lets you monitor your progress. That is difficult to do in your head.

In addition, when you write out your goals you may notice that they evolve or change over time. Perhaps in your initial enthusiasm you wanted to, say, dance in a show on Broadway. Well, a decision like that obviously calls for some life-altering persistence, not to mention extra lessons and exercise, and would most likely mean a major lifestyle change—like moving to New York for auditions. If you plot these things out carefully in your writing, you will soon notice if your goal now seems to aim too high, if it is still realistic, or if it has moved out of line with what you want to put into it.

Along with helping you concentrate on the actual attainment of your goal, your journal is a safe place to examine the more emotional aspects of your wish, such as accepting criticism and rejection and allowing for improvement. As you follow the progress of your goals in journal form, you will be able to monitor your achievements, alter your course, if need be, stay pumped up about your ambition, and reward yourself in relation to the task accomplished. In essence, you are creating an environment for change.

Q: Why is there so much emphasis on self-esteem and writing to the "child within"? I don't remember much about my childhood, and I feel funny writing what I like about myself.

A: There is a power to self-esteem that has its roots in the very center of who you are. You have received many messages about yourself in the course of your life, and some of them may not be in your best interest. When was the last time a friend or family member told you how great you were, and how much you mattered to him or her? Everyone needs more of this kind of nurturing talk. You may have many people who love you—your spouse, your family, your associates—but this is all hollow, if you do not love yourself. You may actually feel unworthy of their love and devotion.

We've all heard the stories: people who seemed to have it all—wealth, success, admiration. One day you find out they have a habitual drug problem or horrible marital difficulties, or they're caught stealing something insignificant. They are like actors wearing a mask, fulfilling the expectations of others but unable to feel good about themselves. Secretly they're empty inside and think of their lives as a sham. Outside influences, praise, the admiration of others: these can neither guarantee nor create good self-esteem.

Writing in a journal provides a very important element in your search for inner peace and meaning. It lets you use your cognitive mind to seek what it is you need. By writing out your thoughts, by putting your urges, wants, and goals into a definable language, you are committing yourself to conscious living, a very definite step toward self-esteem.

Q: Why does my handwriting change over time? Sometimes the style is different from page to page.

A: James W. Pennebaker, a psychologist and teacher at SMU suggests there is evidence of a *letting-go* kind of change when someone writes about deep feelings. This change shows itself by a definite shift in handwritten script styles, and it usually happens when writers finally come to terms with a pressing problem. In his book *Opening Up The Healing Power of Confiding in Others*, Pennebaker writes, "Often, handwriting switches from block to cursive and back to block lettering within the same essay as the writers switch from one topic to another. Similar changes can be seen in the slant of the letters, pen pressure, markouts, and general neatness as a function of topic."

He also cites, through carefully studied observations, evidence of another curious occurrence. When someone talks or writes about an upsetting experience without censoring what she thinks, two conflicting points of view are often exposed. At some time during her explanation of a problem, without her actually being aware of it, the person's thoughts shift in transition from a seemingly benign topic to a distinct venting of anger. For example, he tells of a college junior who wrote,

I love my parents. We have a perfect family life. My parents support me in whatever I do. I wouldn't change anything about my childhood, really . . . [then in the same essay] *My father has been such a bastard, I know that he has something going with his secretary. My mother takes it out on me. I have to wear clothes she wants, date the boy she wants.*

Try to be aware of subtle changes, contradictions, or paradoxes in your narration—and take notice. If examined carefully, they may hold deeper truths, revealing more than you originally thought you were telling.

Q: A friend of mine has just lost her daughter in a terrible accident. I find it difficult to talk to her; should I suggest she journal-write?

A: The loss of a child is a significant trauma. Rather than suggesting journal writing to your friend, you might buy her a copy of this book and let her check it out in her own good time. Different people have different ways of coping with death, and your suggestion may not be right for her needs right now.

Q: Sometimes when I begin to explain a situation or something that's happened to me in my journal, I find myself making excuses for why I'm not at fault. Is this wrong?

A. In an article for *Psychology Today* (June 1989) writer Nick Jordan says that ". . . recent research shows that people who offer themselves plausible excuses have greater self-esteem and better health and perform better on all sorts of cognitive, social, and physical tasks than individuals who put blame on themselves when things go wrong."

If your excuses ultimately provide a higher truth (recognizing that you are making excuses is a good sign), and if you feel you can view your excuses as a temporary outlet, it's quite normal. One of a human being's strongest urges is his self-preservation device.

Having said that, try to be non-judgmental in your journal. Keep in mind that this is a private place for you to confer with your feelings and eventually to discover a deeper logic.

Q: I can't seem to get things going—anything. I can't stand it when people tell me I'm just in a slump, but most times I feel like I'll never be able to finish anything. What can journal writing do to help someone like me?

A: The first real consideration is *Do you know what you want?* Not what your mother wants for you (to be a doctor); not what your wife wants from you (to be rich); not what your boss wants from you (more hours) . . . you get the picture. We are forever being bombarded by others' desires and expectations. The first and most valuable goal, then, is to define what *you* want.

Since your journal is private, it offers you a perfect forum for sorting out how you feel about where you're headed—and, more importantly, where you really want to point your ship. Begin by looking at these two questions and deciding where you really want to be going. Once you know what it is you long for, write it down and look at it frequently. You might copy your goals out of your journal and tape them over your desk or paste them inside your calendar for reinforcement. When a certain step toward a goal is realized, reward yourself with a small gift or pleasure and write in your journal about how achieving your goal makes you feel.

Organization can be learned. It just requires desire, effort, and some time. Maybe you don't really want to accomplish what everyone thinks is best for you. If that's so, don't be afraid of wanting to be average.

Q: What does it mean when I write that I'd like to bop someone or that I wish they'd drop out of sight? Is it sick to wish someone else harm?

A: Carl Jung wrote about the hidden side of our personalities, the part we would rather not claim: he called it "the shadow." As young children, we had certain feelings and emotions that, once expressed, we soon found out were not acceptable. Our parents frowned on natural, but antisocial, behaviors. When we discovered that our parents didn't like this part of us, we suppressed conducts involving aggression, independence, self-indulgence, and other perceived negatives.

When these shadow feelings appear in your writing, you will most likely feel uncomfortable with them. Sometimes the traits we criticize in others may be the very traits we most dislike in ourselves, and in this case our negative feelings may be especially intense. Identify and accept the fact that we all possess these feelings at some time or another. It is part of the maturation process to experience these thoughts, but the mature person does not take action on harmful or violent urges.

Robert A. Johnson, author of *Owning Your Own Shadow* says, "You may draw it, sculpt it, write a vivid story about it, dance it, burn something, or bury it—anything that gives expression to that material without doing damage." He writes, "The unconscious cannot tell the difference between a 'real act' and a symbolic one."

If you cannot forget about your negative feelings, think you are becoming severely distressed, or feel helplessly obsessive about your instincts, please seek outside help from a licensed professional psychologist or psychiatrist.

Q: Why do I feel bad immediately after writing truthfully?

A: Much attention has been devoted to the debilitating effects of repressed feelings and repeated stress on one's health and well-being. But by the same token, bringing secrets and painful thoughts out into the open affects your mood and, consequently, changes the way your body feels initially. You may feel fatigued.

Psychologist and researcher James W. Pennebaker, who has conducted many tests on inhibitions with his students at Southern Methodist University in Dallas, says that, although you may feel sad or depressed shortly after writing, such negative feelings usually dissipate within an hour or so. In rare cases the bad feelings may last for a day or two, but the overwhelming majority of subjects tested "report feelings of relief, happiness, and contentment soon after the writing studies are concluded." He adds that with deeply felt emotions or traumas as the result of death or a tragedy, you will not feel better after writing, but you should come away with a better understanding of your feelings and emotions.

Q: Can someone write in their journal too much?

A: It is difficult to say what you might mean by "too much." Let's look at this question from another perspective. Is your writing about a problem a substitute for taking action? If your journal helps you to organize your thoughts with a positive objective in mind, such as changing what you can change, confronting or talking with someone else, or putting your desires into language, it is serving its purpose.

If your journal becomes a vehicle for complaint; if it is a one-sided dimension of your life, an excuse for venting that will neither help you nor make you feel better, it will lead you nowhere.

Writing is not intended to take the place of companionship and human interaction. Part of your search for purpose should involve your relationships and the pleasure of communicating with co-workers, family, and friends.

Q: Could you explain "venting"?

A: Venting is a temporary state in which strong emotions are released by forceful speaking or writing. The idea is to pass through this emotional release and move on to more constructive thoughts. Lingering there may actually become harmful. When complaining becomes a compulsion, it causes duress and ceases to serve a purpose.

Q: I'd like to do something that's fun to keep me fixed on a long-term goal. I find I lose interest in things I need to do but that take a long time to accomplish. Is there a writing technique for me?

A: Every month, save a whole page in your journal for making up your own horoscope. If you have small tasks that you can accomplish in one month's time, put them in a celestial forecast. It doesn't matter that they are not based on actual star-gazing; the main thing is that you will still be outlining your goal. For example, an Aries could write: It is now time to accept the risk of being yourself. Unique opportunities will present themselves this month . . . (you fill in the rest).

Read your journal horoscope often during the month, just as you might read the horoscope in your favorite magazine. Except that this one will be much more personal and definitely more self-driven!

Q: Can I expect good health benefits from journal writing?

A: In the first place, as any good mental health professional will tell you, symptoms such as heart palpitations, shortness of breath, or problems in sleeping should first be investigated by a medical doctor, preferably by means of a complete physical and neurological examination. Symptoms akin to an anxiety disorder may actually have their basis in another disease, such as a thyroid condition, an allergy, or some other physical ailment. If adverse physical symptoms are definitely shown to be the result of emotional stress, then you can certainly expect your journal writing to have a therapeutic effect—depending on how you use it.

Q: My mother, who is in her sixties, surprised me by saying she would like to keep a journal. Are there writing exercises she can do to keep her mind active?

A: Yes there are, and good for your mother for wanting to know about them!

She may find it pleasant to recall and describe a person who has had an effect on her life. The description should be so accurate that someone reading the characterization would be able to recognize the subject on sight, even though they have never met. This requires some planning—maybe several lists or time lines, and perhaps a few old photographs or mementos to help jog her memory.

If nostalgia is not her thing but she is an avid reader, she might enjoy writing critiques. This actually requires no special training—just opinions. She could write about books or current news events, compose a "letter to the Editor," or whatever she feels like.

In evaluating a book or novel, she might discuss what

makes the book special and what light, if any, it sheds on her own life. Would she have reacted to events in the same way as the main character, or could the situation have been handled better? What are the book's flaws? If she was disappointed in the book, yet felt compelled to finish it, why did she stay with it?

If you are hoping that your mother will write her life story, bear in mind that this is a rather ambitious project for someone starting out. You can encourage her, however, by being more specific. In your first journal, write out a list of questions that you have always wanted to ask your mother about an event or decision in her life. You might ask what her childhood home looked like, what she did as a teenager, who her favorite friends were, how she decided to get married.

Once you get embroiled in this quest, you will find that there are many questions you would like answered. Perhaps some family mysteries will finally be cleared up. If your mother does leave her thoughts and writings to you, they could be a wonderful legacy.

Q: In magazine articles about self-help, the author or doctor always seems to suggest that readers "write something out." What is it about writing that helps?

A: Writing is a form of expression not unlike singing or dancing. In singing you expel emotions through your vocal tones, breath control, and delivery style; in dance you release energy and feelings through movement. Writing can have similar benefits.

Our minds, moreover, have a desire to order things. Even intense feelings and emotions, though we might feel confused by them at first or find them hard to put into words, can be sorted out in the process of putting thoughts and perceptions down on paper. In organizing them, we take charge. The act of ordering our thoughts helps us to release them.

Having written down our questions, we are free, if we choose, to let go of them. We can rid our minds of those problems and concentrate on other matters. Or, if we prefer to look at those issues further, the language is there in concrete terms to be reordered or to serve as a basis for future action. We can even make use of a strong symbolic gesture and tear up what has been written.

Q: I thought that I was over my divorce, but whenever I sit down to write in my journal I keep dredging up painful feelings about the past. Am I obsessing? Is there a way never to feel like this again?

A: It's difficult to move on after a troubling situation. If you have been depressed for more than a few weeks, you might check to see whether you have a health problem. If you are physically OK but you keep thinking about your situation, try to set up a dialogue with your problem. The unsent letter might be your best technique. Don't hedge or worry about writing raw feelings; it won't help you to hold them in.

Later, ask yourself whether you have some lingering guilt. Do you believe you could have changed the situation, or that there was more you could have done? Is this belief realistic? Is there a reason you want to blame yourself—maybe something that happened in the past that feels similar to what you feel now? Try not to beat yourself up.

A change of perspective can help. You don't need to draw sweeping conclusions about how you will live the rest of your life, but do try writing about some changes you'd like to bring about. What have you learned? Write until you have exhausted your feelings. If necessary, repeat this process until you feel you've said everything that could be said. Still later, look back. What has changed?

Q: I've heard the word "mindfulness" used recently. Does this have anything to do with journal writing?

A: Yes, very much so. Mindfulness means that the way you think about things has a great effect on what happens to you, such as changes in your physical condition. Physicians call this "psychoneuroimmunology"—the study of

how what goes on in our minds, our emotions and atti-
tudes affects our health. Mental clarity and the sense that
we are in control of decisions that affect us are powerfully
involved with our physical well-being, as many are coming
to believe. This is why journal writing can be an effective
tool for health.

Q: What do you think is the most difficult feeling to overcome?

A: Aside from debilitating fears and the effects of personal
traumas, such as health problems or bereavement, I would
have to say that false expectations present the greatest
challenges. When someone wants something she cannot
get, it forces her to ask "Why?" Her mind sets about trying
to find reasons for her defeat. Blaming others sets up a cycle of anger and resentment; or the person may ask such
self-defeating questions as, "Am I being punished?" This is
a futile exercise if expectations were out of line in the first
place, and may lead the person to set herself up as a victim.

From the suffering viewpoint of the victim, life is filled
with uncertainty and disappointment. "Nothing will ever
change. Nothing good ever happens to me." If disillu-
sioned thinking lasts too long, the person may even become convinced that her defeated expectations were the
result of something set against her deliberately. What a
horrible cycle of despair this creates once a mind has
closed. It is a hard road to come back from. And yet the
simple truth is that not all things can be granted to us; nor
is life always fair. By learning to accept this in our own
lives, we can free ourselves from much that holds us back.

Chapter 9

Conclusions

"The hours of a wise man are lengthened by
his ideas."
— JOSEPH ADDISON, *The Spectator*

You have learned so much throughout the course of this book. Your
journal is now uniquely a product of you. It is a powerful document
because it contains ideas, desires, struggles, questions, pain, truth,
despair, and humor. All of these feelings are an imprint of your essence on paper.

In the beginning you made decisions about choosing and personalizing your book. You selected the right cover and size, the
most comfortable implement to write with. You figured out the best
time to purge your mind of its thoughts. You have experimented
with different writing exercises, exercises in which you were able to
make use of your own dynamics. Did you adapt the questions and
make them yours?

You took the initiative to make subjective sense out of all the
chaotic messages that are thrust on you in the course of the day, and
you lined them out in your book in your own self-language. Then,
armed with a better understanding, you discovered a new way, perhaps a more creative way, of looking at and confronting outward cir-
cumstances.

In the chapters dealing with seeking and examining you have
been shown how to center in on what you think. You sought to find

out what you believe, or did believe in; practiced separating personal myth from fact. You learned to write word portraits about the people who circle around you in your daily life, seeking to make realistic assessments about your role and your relation to them.

Now, every time you complete a quiz or questionnaire in a magazine or flyer, you will think about pasting it into your journal as a signpost of what you thought and how you felt about that subject. Date all your entries, won't you? Maybe you've never answered that question before. It will be interesting to see how your answer changes over time.

In the section on tapping the creative unconscious, you have learned more about meditation and its beneficial effects. You thought about, and imagined, seeing yourself from different vantage points, above and within. You asked to remember what you dreamed while asleep, and you created new waking dreams with your visualizations during the day.

You are not intimidated by taking an idea as far as it will go, because now you know how to cluster. You won't feel silly about drawing or loosening up to begin writing, or about playing with symbols and free association when the mood suggests it.

You should have a better awareness of what it is you need: self-love, attention to your health, time, space—and what the story is you want to write. You know you don't need to write your life's story all at once, or tell absolutely everything. But you have a method, a system that will help you to see the larger picture and where you fit in. You will be able to benefit your ambitions with a clearer sense of direction, and you now have another outlet to help you to accept what you cannot change.

You know much more about transitions now and what you can do to calm yourself during the "between times" when you shift from one role to another. You want to have a full life, not a life where you are simply waiting for happiness or for good things to happen to you.

Candle Concentration in the chapter on Venting, Realizing, and Coping gave you another way to calm anxious moments. You learned to talk back to worry in the form of *Unsent Letters*. *Key Words* and *Lists* will help you get back in focus when your job efforts seem overwhelming or uncertain. You are much less likely to get sidetracked when misfortune strikes, and if you become dumbfounded for a time, you can find strength and seek the inherent lesson in the process of healing.

You have no need to control all things because you don't need to be afraid. *Time Reference* and *Stories* encourage you to tame your fears, though you realize through continued practice that overcoming fears will take time and effort—and sometimes professional counseling. No man or woman is an island, and everyone has need of support and confidence from others occasionally.

Continue to tackle those writing skills that help you to see your inherent value and self-worth, enabling you to discount cruel childhood labels. You will want to stand up to your negative self-talk by writing self-portraits and kind affirmations frequently. Everyone's confidence sinks and rises with the troubles and blows that they take and survive. Reaffirm your own worth by looking for ways to be kind to yourself, to nurture your best talents.

When illness strikes, the devices of *Distance, Distraction,* and *Creating Alternate Worlds* can help you fend off the pain and confusion. I hope you will be able to cultivate a renewed sense of humor after tragedy. Work at it, because that is a healing signpost.

If you wrote a conversation with your troubles or questions, did it bring answers or relief? Did it help bridge the loneliness that comes with loss? Keep up with your writing; you may need more time to find a sense of closure. Not everyone weathers loss in predictable ways. Some people bounce back from losses quicker than others. Tell yourself you are coping, and that a better day will come with time.

Try to focus on noticing something new about the day. Allow change to touch your life. Without surprise, without curiosity for new skills and the adapting that comes with newness, there is no possibility for growth. And growth is essential to a complete life.

Your journal gave you new tools for apportioning your time. With imagination and rehearsal, you established a program for planning new goals. The device known as *Time Line* let you take a long-term perspective of your available years and plan for them. You can also use the time line, remember, to monitor goals—to frame ideas you once longed for and have somehow forgotten. Make these goals difficult to ignore. You know that hard work and achieving a goal in a challenging area are what equip you to handle success and failure. Attainable plans provide new ideas, new latitude with which to explore alternate sources for satisfaction, allowing you to remain excited and fulfilled.

New avenues of family communication were explored using scrapbook ideas, surveys, and individual question methods. You may have created a family memoir or started a new family biography.

You want to know that you can return to childhood memories, and you have discovered some triggers for cultivating a communion with the child you once were. In your journal you can play around with these techniques; you may discover some surprising memories, once you ask for them.

Acceptance is your new watchword as you move deeper in your introspection and begin to see universal traits in yourself and others. You want to be able to identify with other human causes and needs. With a guide to watch over your own mental health, you have less need for assurances or acceptance from outside, and that makes you feel more confident and assured. With quiet journal reflection you have had time to think about a purpose—what essence of you will remain when you are gone. If you have not already done so, compose a personal testimony to leave your family. In an article about legacy for *Writer's Digest* called "Power Lounging" (February 1993), writer Gregg Levoy observed, ". . . obituaries are little more than posthumous resumés: books authored, titles held, military ranks attained, degrees earned. They are summary statements of our lives, testaments to what we hold in esteem. And there are no hallelujahs for idleness, for time spent with family, for afternoons given over to long, dreamy walks." Confessed workaholics like Levoy find that the busyness of doing, doing, doing comes at the expense of feeling and examining feelings. We need to connect with ourselves, to create a space so that we can, as Levoy says "hold that silence up to my ears, like an empty shell, and listen to the roar of my own life." The journal offers a means to discover what non-material gifts you offer.

Chapters 7 and 8 gave you an assortment of skills to turn your journal into an individual, cathartic support system. You have the ability to tap into your spirituality, your sexuality, and your hidden feelings. You are practicing exercises and answering questions that will help you continue to cope, to make decisions, and to rely on the marvelous person you are.

Proof that *everything is within you* continues to manifest itself in all the different ways you express yourself in journal writing. Although this idea is most commonly associated with Eastern disciplines and methodology, its theories are based on principles that we in the West take for granted, such as intuition, common sense, and the urge to do what is right. Mindfulness, consciously thinking and seeking information about the way you live and acting on it, can be a source of health and wholeness if you make use of it.

Continue your search for personal truth, and keep in mind these basic guidelines:

Details. Your brain, a creative problem-solving device, enjoys filling in details. Discount nothing. Deny nothing. Everything you think is valuable and evolving. Make things whole. The more personal information you have, the more you will feel that nothing is missing.

Emotions. Find different ways to express your emotions. If you feel blocked by confusion, think of your strong belief or thought as a flow of energy that leaves your head and travels down your arm and into your fingers, finding its outlet through the pen and out onto paper. How does it feel to let it go this way?

Conversation. Write as if in conversation. No need to feel stilted and formal in your journal. Remember, there is no one to judge grammar or syntax. Your unique voice will emerge in writing just as you have learned to communicate with friends.

Memories. Balance your questions with memories of similar experiences. Has this happened in the past? How did you handle it then? If you consider this perspective, you will see that you have already overcome and learned much in your lifetime.

Senses. Use comparisons and contrasts. If you first know what something is not, the chance of finding what it means to you is greater. Imagine yourself floating up above and looking at yourself down below. Writing out your emotions and perceptions helps you keep your attention focused on a problem longer.

The most wonderful thing about a journal is that it will never put demands on you. If you forget to write, it will not scold you. It is always waiting patiently for your return. If you write only during the crisis times in your life, so be it. The journal is always ready to serve as an outlet for your emotions and feelings. If it helps you to adapt positively and safely, that is reason enough to keep it around.

Your journal is a place to tell secrets. It will not betray your confidence or tell anything you do not want shared. It is non-judgmental. It allows you to scream between the covers. It lets you examine your decisions and does not reprove you when you make mistakes.

The journal is a loving ear, a place for you to figure out that you are worth more than material possessions, social status, and outward appearances. If you let it, it will help you to define your own personal integrity.

Take comfort in your writing. It is something you have control over even when the world around you seems to be falling apart. You can learn to find new ways not only to express yourself but to nurture those who depend on you. You can attempt to understand what it is you need and to convey that to others who love and nurture you.

If your journal helps you to meditate, to slow your life's rhythms and to celebrate now, it will be the best calendar you will ever own. You may well make two thousand acquaintances in the course of your lifetime. Will you know and remember who they are? More importantly, will you know how they have affected your life? Learn what there is to learn and discard the rest. If mystery is your answer to some of life's questions, you won't have to obsess about what could or should or won't be. Letting go is something you can learn to do when you need to.

Your journal is an eyewitness to your history. It has stopped you long enough to say, "I'm here. I'm thinking and growing and trying to figure it all out." It remains where you left it, an extension of you, conveying all the language you can muster and leave in it. You have this vehicle. You have a friend. You have you.

Appendix

Thoughts to Write by

I never travel without my diary. One should
always have something sensational to read in
the train.

— OSCAR WILDE

To journal writers like myself, quotations are synonymous with inspiration. And in comparison to that of someone longing for a
sweet and picking up a solitary raisin, a single taste (like, perhaps,
the quote above) demands a handful. On the following pages, then,
are several handfuls. There are a number of categories here. If you
find yourself stuck in your journal writing, you may wish to review
one or more of these for some fresh thoughts on dealing with the
issue at hand.

Adapting

Greatness of soul consists not so much in soaring high and in pressing forward, as in knowing how to adapt and limit oneself.
— MONTAIGNE

One must change one's tactics every ten years if one wishes to maintain one's superiority.
— NAPOLEON I

Times change, and we change with them.
— ANONYMOUS

The mere process of growing old together will make the slightest acquaintance seem a bosom-friend.
— LOGAN PEARSALL SMITH

I don't use any method. I'm from the let's pretend school of acting.
— HARRISON FORD

Anger

I bear no grudges. My heart is as big as the sky and I have a mind that retains absolutely nothing.
— BETTE MIDLER

The best way to convince a fool that he is wrong is to let him have his own way.
— JOSH BILLINGS, pseudonym of HENRY WHEELER SHAW

We are all born mad. Some remain so.
— SAMUEL BECKETT

I never work better than when I am inspired by anger; when I am angry, I can write, pray, and preach well, for then my whole temperament is quickened, my understanding sharpened, and all mundane vexations and temptations depart.
— MARTIN LUTHER

Anybody can become angry—that is easy; but to be angry with the right person, and to the right degree, and at the right time, and for the right purpose, and in the right way—that is not within everybody's power and is not easy.
— ARISTOTLE

Anxiety

Do not push forward a wagon; you will only raise the dust about yourself. Do not think of all your anxieties; you will only make yourself ill.
— SHIH KING

Grief is a species of idleness.
— SAMUEL JOHNSON

The mistake which is commonly made about neurotics is to suppose that they are interesting. It is not interesting to be always unhappy, engrossed with oneself, ungrateful and malignant, and never quite in touch with reality.
— CYRIL CONNOLLY

The vast majority of our words and deeds are unnecessary. Eliminate them, and how much toil and trouble will vanish with them! Therefore, on every occasion, let's ask ourselves, "Is this necessary?"
— MARCUS AURELIUS

I'm not into character assassination, except my own.
— CARRIE FISHER

Beliefs

I read books like mad, but I am careful not to let anything I read influence me.
— MICHAEL CAINE

When we got into office, the thing that surprised me was to find that things were just as bad as we'd been saying they were.
— JOHN F. KENNEDY

I arise in the morning torn between a desire to improve (or save) the world and a desire to enjoy (or savor) the world. This makes it hard to plan the day.
— E.B. WHITE

A prejudice is a vagrant opinion without visible means of support.
— AMBROSE BIERCE

I respect faith, but doubt is what gets you an education.
— WILSON MIZNER

"One *can't* believe impossible things."

"I daresay you haven't had much practice," said the Queen. "When I was your age, I always did it for half-an-hour a day. Why, sometimes I've believed as many as six impossible things before breakfast."
— LEWIS CARROLL

Childhood

There may be some doubt as to who are the best people to have charge of children, but there can be no doubt that parents are the worst.
— GEORGE BERNARD SHAW

I am a spy in the house of me. I report back from the front lines of the battle that is me. I am somewhat nonplussed by the event that is my life.
— CARRIE FISHER

There is always one moment in childhood when the door opens and lets the future in.
— GRAHAM GREENE

I sucked in chisels and hammers with my nurse's milk.
— MICHELANGELO

You have to ask children and birds how cherries and strawberries taste.
— GOETHE

Creativity

In the creative state a man is taken out of himself. He lets down as it were a bucket into his subconscious, and draws up something which is normally beyond his reach. He mixes this thing with his normal experiences, and out of the mixture he makes a work of art.
— E.M. FORSTER

When it came to writing about wine, I did what almost everybody else does—faked it.
— ART BUCHWALD

A poet can survive everything but a misprint.
— OSCAR WILDE

What I needed was what people so obliquely refer to as space, a distance from what was pressing in on me, a penetrating quiet inside. And I needed to hold that silence up to my ears, like an empty shell, and listen to the roar of my own life.
— GREGG LEVOY

Dreams

Sometimes in my dreams there are women. When such dreams happen, immediately I remember: "I am a monk."
— THE DALAI LAMA

You see things; and you say, "Why?" But I dream things that never were; and I say, "Why not?"
— GEORGE BERNARD SHAW

Nina: Your play's hard to act. There are no living people in it.
Treplev: Living people! We should show life neither as it is nor as it ought to be, but as we see it in our dreams.
— ANTON CHEKHOV, *The Seagull*

Existence would be intolerable if we were never to dream.
— ANATOLE FRANCE

Fear

Am I afraid of high notes? Of course I am afraid! What sane man is not?
— LUCIANO PAVAROTTI

"The trouble is, Sancho," said Don Quixote, "you are so afraid that you cannot see or hear properly; for one of the effects of fear is to disturb the senses and cause things to appear other than what they are."
— MIGUEL DE CERVANTES

Fear comes from uncertainty. When we are absolutely certain, whether of our worth or worthlessness, we are almost impervious to fear. Thus a feeling of utter unworthiness can be a source of courage.
— ERIC HOFFER

I'm originally from Iowa. It took a long time for me to realize we were free to go.
— JAKE JOHANNSEN

Goals and Ambitions

I want everybody in the United States to be very highly educated, to have super taste. I mean, people say, "But aren't you an elitist?" and I say, "Yes, but I want everybody to be an elitist."
— PAUL FUSSELL

I have most of my life been miserably conscious that I am not the average Englishman. Let no one think I say this with self-satisfaction, for I think that there is nothing better than to be like everybody else. It is the only way to be happy, and it is with but a wry face that one tells oneself that happiness is not everything.
— W. SOMERSET MAUGHAM

Do not wish to be anything but what you are, and try to be that perfectly.
— ST. FRANCIS DE SALES

He who follows another sees nothing, learns nothing, nay, seeks nothing.
— SIR WILLIAM OSLER

One always has to spoil a picture a little bit, in order to fix it.
— EUGENE DELACROIX

If I had not been born Peron, I would have liked to be Peron.
— JUAN PERON

Listening

Accustom thyself to attend carefully to what is said by another, and as much as it is possible be in the speaker's mind.
— MARCUS AURELIUS

The only way to entertain some folks is to listen to them.
— KIN HUBBARD

Do you think I can listen all day to such stuff? Be off, or I'll kick you downstairs.
— LEWIS CAROLL

Even the best writers talk too much.
— LUC DE VAUVENARGUES

The man who listens to Reason is lost: Reason enslaves all whose minds are not strong enough to master her.
— GEORGE BERNARD SHAW

It is the province of knowledge to speak and it is the privilege of wisdom to listen.
— OLIVER WENDELL HOLMES

Loneliness

In Genesis it says that it is not good for a man to be alone, but sometimes it is a great relief.
　　— JOHN BARRYMORE

Be not afraid of life. Believe that life *is* worth living, and your belief will help create the fact.
　　— WILLIAM JONES

A man can be himself only so long as he is alone; and, if he does not love solitude, he will not love freedom; for it is only when he is alone that he is really free.
　　— ARTHUR SCHOPENHAUER

A lonely impulse of delight
Drove to this tumult in the clouds . . .
　　— W.B. YEATS

I was taught to feel, perhaps too much,
The self-sufficing power of solitude.
　　— WILLIAM WORDSWORTH

Memories

God gave us our memories so that we might have roses in December.
— JAMES MATTHEW BARRIE

The only thing I ever said to my parents when I was a teenager was "Hang up, I got it!"
— CAROL LEIFER

Nothing changes more constantly than the past; for the past that influences our lives does not consist of what actually happened, but of what men believe happened.
— GERALD W. JOHNSON

What once was thought can never be undone.
— FRIEDRICH DURRENMATT

There comes a time in a man's life and I've had many of them.
— CASEY STENGEL

Mistakes

When I make a mistake, it's a beaut.
— FIORELLO LAGUARDIA

All great men make mistakes.
— WINSTON CHURCHILL

How hard it is to confess that we have spoken without thinking, that we have talked nonsense. How many a man says a thing in haste and heat, without fully understanding or half meaning it, and then, because he has said it, holds fast to it, and tries to defend it as if it were true! But how much wiser, how much more admirable and attractive, it is when man has the grace to perceive and acknowledge his mistakes! It gives us assurance that he is capable of learning, of growing, of improving, so that his future will be better than his past.
— HENRY VAN DYKE

I made my mistakes, but in all my years of public life I have never profited from public service. I have earned every cent.
— RICHARD NIXON

Others

Friends are the thermometers by which one may judge the temperature of our fortunes.
— MARGUERITE, COUNTESS OF BLESSINGTON

The old believe everything, the middle-aged suspect everything, the young know everything.
— OSCAR WILDE

It is well, when one is judging a friend, to remember that he is judging you with the same godlike and superior impartiality.
— ARNOLD BENNETT

Admiration: our polite recognition of another man's resemblance to ourselves.
—AMBROSE BIERCE

I have often wondered how it is that every man loves himself more than all the rest of men, but yet sets less value on his own opinion of himself than on the opinion of others.
— MARCUS AURELIUS

Patience and Commitment

Do not believe that your enthusiasm will be a light always burning. You must have oil in your lamps. You must know that study and patient labor are indispensable even to genius. God may have given you genius, but unless he has also given you industry, the genius will leak away, unused, wasted, without profit. Inspiration, intuition and all efflorenscence of genius are divine gifts; yet there must be some material for them to work upon. You cannot have a flame unless there is something that will feed combustion.
— HENRY WARD BEECHER

Patience, and shuffle the cards.
— MIGUEL DE CERVANTES

A man's work, whether in music, painting or literature, is always a portrait of himself.
— ALDOUS HUXLEY

Stew Nugent has decided to go to work till he can find something better.
— KIN HUBBARD

The difference between involvement and commitment? Think ham and eggs. The chicken was involved, the pig was committed.
— RITA MAE BROWN

Peace

When we do not find peace of mind in ourselves it is useless to look for it elsewhere.
— Duc Francois de La Rochefoucauld

Happiness and success depend strangely upon our ability to free our minds to work for us. Anything that inhibits the flow of spiritual energy through the mind tends to defeat us. A careful and consistent cultivation of a relaxed attitude is important. You do not need to be defeated by anything. Your life can be a great experience. Get the calm, selective ability to take up one thing at a time and concentrate upon it. Deal finally with it, if possible, before passing on to the next matter.
— Norman Vincent Peale

At sixteen I was stupid, confused, insecure and indecisive. At twenty-five I was wise, self-confident, prepossessing and assertive. At forty-five I am stupid, confused, insecure and indecisive. Who would have supposed that maturity is only a short break in adolescence?
— Jules Feiffer

Principles

The real significance of crime is in its being a breach of faith
with the community of mankind.
— JOSEPH CONRAD

There is nothing so bad or so good that you will not find an
Englishman doing it, but you will never find an Englishman in
the wrong. He does everything on principle. He fights you on
patriotic principles; he robs you on business principles; he
enslaves you on imperial principles.
— GEORGE BERNARD SHAW

A cause may be inconvenient, but it's magnificent. It's like
champagne or high shoes, and one must be prepared to suffer
for it.
— ARNOLD BENNETT

You can construct the character of a man and his age not only
from what he does and says, but from what he fails to say and do.
— NORMAN DOUGLAS

It is better to stir up a question without deciding it, than to
decide it without stirring it up.
— JOSEPH JOUBERT

Realization

In order to know what is an aberration you must know what is normal. In order to know what is in excess you must know what is the true measure. Who can tell whether a man is selfish unless he knows what is benevolent? Who can tell whether a man has departed from the correct idea unless he has some conception of that idea? The very foundation on which we stand necessitates knowledge of man as its chief basis.
— HENRY WARD BEECHER

There's something about a closet that makes a skeleton terribly restless.
— JOHN BARRYMORE

In the struggle for self-realization a few men become artists. They learn the possibilities of the materials with which they deal: they put themselves into fruitful relations with the things which can nourish, the forces which can inspire them. And they put forth the creative energy that is in them freely and continuously.
— HAMILTON WRIGHT MABIE

A virtue which I need in a higher degree, to give beauty and lustre to my behaviour, is gentleness. If I had more of an air of gentleness I should be much mended.
— JONATHAN EDWARDS

Relaxation

Practice lifting your mind above the confusion around you. One way is to form mental pictures of great hills or mountain ranges, the wide sweep of ocean, some green valley spreading out below you. You can even hear skylarks if you listen carefully.
  — NORMAN VINCENT PEALE

There is no joy but calm!
  — ALFRED, LORD TENNYSON

A man becomes aware of his life's flow
And hears its winding murmur; and he sees
The meadows where it glides, the sun, the breeze.
And there arrives a lull in the hot race
Wherein he doth forever chase
That flying and elusive shadow, rest.
An air of coolness plays upon his face,
And an unwonted calm pervades his breast.
And then he thinks he knows
The hills where his life rose,
And the sea where it goes.
  — MATTHEW ARNOLD

Go drink tea.
  — ZEN MASTER SEUNG SAHN

Self-esteem

We are all worms. But I do believe that I am a glow-worm.
— WINSTON CHURCHILL

If I only had a little humility I would be perfect.
— TED TURNER

I'm not handsome in the classical sense. The eyes droop, the mouth is crooked, the teeth aren't straight, the voice sounds like a mafioso pallbearer, but somehow it all works.
— SYLVESTER STALLONE

In my own mind, I am still a fat brunette from Toledo, and I always will be.
— GLORIA STEINEM

In each human heart are a tiger, a pig, an ass, and a nightingale; diversity of character is due to their unequal activity.
— AMBROSE BIERCE

I'm the Connie Francis of rock 'n' roll.
— ELTON JOHN

Success

I am the most spontaneous speaker in the world because every word, every gesture, and every retort has been carefully rehearsed.
— GEORGE BERNARD SHAW

I'm a publisher because it's a cover for my indulgence. I love to read all day. But I come from nice Puritan stock, and I grew up believing that you have to work all day, so I made reading my work.
— ANN GETTY

I do not try to dance better than anyone else. I only try to dance better than myself.
— MIKHAIL BARYSHNIKOV

Be nice to people on your way up because you'll need them on your way down.
— WILSON MIZNER

I have trouble with toast. Toast is very difficult. You have to watch it all the time or it burns up.
— JULIA CHILD

Truth

The inquiry of truth, which is the lovemaking or wooing of it; the knowledge of truth, which is the praise of it; and the belief of truth, which is the enjoying of it, is the sovereign good of human nature.
— FRANCIS BACON

When a man comes to me for advice, I find out what kind of advice he wants, and I give it to him.
— JOSH BILLINGS, pseudonym of HENRY WHEELER SHAW

It is unfortunate, considering that enthusiasm moves the world, that so few enthusiasts can be trusted to speak the truth.
— ARTHUR JAMES, EARL OF BALFOUR

Nature makes only dull animals; we owe the fool to society.
— HONORE DE BALZAC

I'm not confused, I'm just well mixed.
— ROBERT FROST

I always thought if you worked hard enough and tried hard enough, things would work out. I was wrong.
— KATHERINE GRAHAM

Wellness

My body is that part of the world that my ideas can change. Even imaginary diseases can become real ones. The rest of the world cannot be disturbed by my notions.
— G.C. LICHTENBERG

Look to your health; and if you have it, praise God, and value it next to a good conscience; for health is the second blessing that we mortals are capable of; a blessing that money cannot buy.
— WALT WHITMAN

There is nothing the body suffers that the soul may not profit by.
— GEORGE MEREDITH

We must always change, renew, rejuvenate ourselves; otherwise we harden.
— JOHANN WOLFGANG VON GOETHE

A man who had not seen Keuner for a long time greeted him with these words: "You haven't changed at all.

"Oh," said Herr Keuner, deeply shocked.
— BERTOLT BRECHT

Writing

A well-written life is almost as rare as a well-spent one.
— THOMAS CARLYLE

There's nothing to writing. All you do is sit down at a typewriter and open a vein.
— WALTER "RED" SMITH

Most writers write books that they wouldn't read. I ought to know; I've done it myself.
— GORE VIDAL

What is written without effort is in general read without pleasure.
— SAMUEL JOHNSON

Good writing is a kind of skating which carries off the performer where he would not go.
— RALPH WALDO EMERSON

Peppe is getting so much smarter. It wasn't so long ago that he used to rip up the *TV Guide*, but now he has graduated to ripping up the *Reader's Digest*.
— ANN IMPERATORE discussing Peppe, a Capuchin monkey.

Alphabetical List of Exercises

Alarm Clock, 91
Banish Childhood Labels, 63-64
Candle Concentration, 57-58
Centering, 31-32
Change Your Point of View,
    94-95
Cluster, 44-45
Creative Problem Solving, 50-51
Decision Help, 97-98
Develop Your Spirituality, 102
Dialogue, 70-71
Dictionary, 49
Doodle, 89-90
Draw, 44-45
Dreams, 46-47
Fact Check, 34-36
Family Journal, 97
Fight Back, 66
Fortify Your Will, 99-102
Free Association, 49-50
How-to Power, 92
Imagery, 43-44
Keeping a Family, 77-78
Key Words, 60
Left Hand/Right Hand, 51
Lists, 33-34, 61
Make a Declaration, 68
Mandalas, 51-52

Master Anger, 64-65
Metaphors, 91
Mood Changers, 98
New Direction, 53
New Edges, 48-49
Ode to Your Body, 95
One Hundred Lists, 96
Organize, 36-37
Personality and Self-portrait,
    37-38, 67
Portraits of Influential People,
    85-86
Priority Review, 92-93
Questionnaire, 38
Realistic List
Reflect, 78-79
Rehearse, 75-76
Reprioritize, 60-61
Self-portrait, 66-67
Squaring Up, 66
Stories, 62-63
Symbols, 52-53
Time Line, 76-77
Time Reference, 62
Tracking Emotions, 90-91
Truth Check, 98-99
Unsent Letters, 59, 95-96
Unstalling, 96-97

Index

Note: for information on specific exercises contained in this book, see the separate listing on page 149.

Ackerman, Diane, 31, 69
Addison, Joseph, 117
To Althea, From Prison, 42
Anxiety, 57
The Art of Time, 73

Baldwin, Christina, 21, 46, 47, 93
Beckett, Samuel, 55
Bereavement, 70
Bilich, Michael, 75
The Book of Questions, 78
The Brain Has a Mind of Its Own, 29
Bringing Up a Moral Child, 65
Brown, Rosellen, 92
Burnout, job-related, 59
Buzan, Tony, 44

Carlyle, Thomas, 29
Case, Joyce, 50-51
Childhood reflection and journal writing, 81-87
Chopra, Deepak, 100
Colson, Charles, 39
Common questions on journal writing, 105-116
Creativity and intuition, 41-54
Creativity in Business, 51, 75

Daily writing, integration of, 22
Death of a loved one, dealing with, 70
Drawing on the Right Side of the Brain, 45
The Dreaming Brain, 46
Dudevant, Aurore Dupin Baroness, 15

Edwards, Betty, 45
Examples of Durations, 73

Fear, confronting, 62
Format selection, 24-25
Frank, Anne, 14-15
Franklin, Benjamin, 34
Freudenberger, Herbert J., 59
Friedman, Lisa, 96

George Sand: A Biography, 15
Gerson, Noel, 15
Gill, Brendan, 85
Goldberg, Vicki, 16
Goulding, Mary McClure, 58

Harris, Lou, 55
Harry S Truman In His Own Words, 16
Here at the New Yorker, 85
Hillman, William, 16

Hobson, J. Allen, 46

Illness, confronting, 67-68
Inside America, 55
Intuition and creativity, 41-54

Job burnout, 59
Johnson, Robert A., 111
Jordan, Nick, 109
Journal, 90
Jung, Carl, 110

Kennedy, John F., 12
Kushner, Rabbi Harold, 95, 102

Leavitt, Harold J., 42
Levoy, Gregg, 120
Lovelace, Richard, 42
Low, Abraham, 97
Lowry, Lois, 34

Magical Mind, Magical Body, 100
*Margaret Bourke-White: A
    Biography*, 16
Martin, Russell, 67
Marx, Groucho, 65
Matters Gray and White, 67
Mekler, Eva, 65
Milton, John, 106
Moore, Judith, 25
Motivation and journal
    keeping, 17-19, 29-39
Myers, Rochelle, 51, 52, 75

Native Son, 81
A Natural History of the Senses,
    31, 69
Necessary Losses, 86
The New Diary, 20, 94

Nin, Anaïs, 25, 76, 85
Not to Worry, 58

One to One, 46-47, 93
Options in journal writing,
    13-27
Owning Your Own Shadow, 111

Pain and illness, confronting,
    67-68
Paradise Lost, 106
Pennebaker, James W., 98-99,
    108
Pepys, Samuel, 14
The Personality Self-portrait, 38
Pritchard, Rev. Edward, 69
Privacy, importance of, 23-24
Progoff, Ira, 47

Questions on journal writing,
    common, 105-116
Questions, as journal material,
    78

Rainer, Tristine, 20, 94
Ray, Michael, 51, 52, 75
Recovery Incorporated, 97
Restak, Richard, 29, 31, 41
Richter, 29
Rico, Gabriele Lusser, 44, 45
Robinson, Elwood, 59
Russianoff, Penelope, 86

Sand, George, 15
Schiller, Friedrich von, 31
Schrieber-Servan, Jean Louis,
    74
Schulman, Michael, 65
Selection of a journal, 19-21
Selection of writing instrument,
    21
Self-esteem, 55-72
Self-examination and journal
    writing, 89-103
Sexuality, 93-94

Socrates, 13
The Spectator, 117
Speigel, Dr. David, 69
Stock, Gregory, 78
Strong, George Templeton, 14

Thoreau, Henry David, 15, 74, 90
Time, passage of, and journal writing, 73-80
Truman, Harry, 16

Viorst, Judith, 86

Weinberger, Daniel, 56
When All You've Ever Wanted Isn't Enough, 95
When Am I Going to Be Happy?, 86
White-Bourke, Margaret, 16
Williams, Dr. Redford, 64
Woolf, Virginia, 16
Worry, 58-59
Wright, Richard, 81
Writer's Digest, 120
Writing instrument, selection of, 21
Writing the Natural Way, 44

Bibliography: Books

Ackerman, Diane. *The Natural History of the Senses*. New York: Random House, 1990.

Adler, Mortimer J. and Charles Van Doren, ed. *Great Treasury of Western Thought*. New York & London: R.R. Bowker Company, 1977.

Asher, Sandy. *Where Do You Get Your Ideas?* New York: Walker Pub. Co., 1987.

Baldridge, Letitia. *The Complete Guide to a Great Social Life*. New York: Rawson Assoc., 1987.

Baldwin, Christina. *One to One: Self-Understanding through Journal Writing*. New York: M. Evans and Co., 1977.

Barry, Joseph. *Infamous Woman: The Life of George Sand*. New York: Doubleday & Co., 1977.

Bentley, Nicolas, ed. *The Treasury of Humorous Quotations*. London: Phoenix House Limited, 1951.

Biffle, Christopher. *A Journey Through Your Childhood*. Los Angeles: Jeremy Tarcher, 1989.

Boswell, John. *The Awful Truth About Publishing*. New York: Warner Books, 1986.

Brande, Dorothea. *On Becoming A Writer*. Los Angeles: Tarcher, 1981.

Brown, Rita Mae. *Starting From Scratch*. New York: Bantam Books, 1988.

Brown, Rosellen. "Don't Just Sit There: Writing as a Polymorphous Perverse Pleasure" *Writers on Writing*. Hanover, NH: University Press of New England, 1991.

Burns, David, D. *Feeling Good: The New Mood Therapy*. New York: Penguin Books, 1981.

Conran, Shirley. *Superwoman.* New York: Crown Pub., 1978.

De Bono, Edward. *New Think: The Use of Lateral Thinking in the Generation of New Ideas.* New York: Basic Books, 1968.

Druck, Ken and James C. Simmons. *The Secrets Men Keep.* Excerpted from *The Fireside Treasury of Light.* New York; Simon & Schuster, 1990.

Dunaway, Philip and Mel Evans, eds. *A Treasury of the World's Greatest Diaries.* New York: Doubleday & Co. Inc., 1957.

Dyer, Wayne. *Your Erroneous Zones.* New York: Funk & Wagnalls, 1976.

Edwards, Betty. *Drawing on the Right Side of the Brain.* Los Angeles: J.P. Tarcher/Houghton Mifflin, 1979.

Frank, Anne, prepared by Ernst Schnabel. *Anne Frank: A Portrait In Courage.* New York: Harcourt, Brace and Co., 1958.

Flesch, Rudolf, ed. *The Book of Unusual Quotations.* New York: Harper & Brothers, 1957.

Gerson, Noel. *George Sand: A Biography of the First Modern, Liberated Woman.* New York: David McKay Co. Inc., 1972.

Gill, Brendan. *Here At The New Yorker.* New York: Random House, 1975.

Harris, Louis. *Inside America.* New York: Vintage Books/Random House, 1987.

Hillman, William. *Harry S Truman In His Own Words.* New York: Bonanza Books and Crown Pub., 1984.

Hobson, J. Allen. *The Dreaming Brain,* Cambridge, MA: Harvard University Press and Basic Books, 1989.

James, Jennifer. *Success is the Quality of Your Journey.* New York: Newmarket Press, 1983.

Jasen, David A. *P.G. Wodehouse: A Portrait of a Master.* New York: Mason & Lipscomb Pub., 1974.

Johnson, Horace, and Helen Johnson ed. *The Bedside Treasury of Inspiration.* Englewood Cliffs, NJ: Prentice-Hall, Inc., 1956.

Katz, Stan J., and Aimee E. Liu. *Success Trap Rethink Your Ambitions.* New York: Ticknor & Fields, 1990.

Kidder, Tracy. *House*, Boston: Houghton Mifflin Co., 1985.

King, Serge Kahili. *Mastering Your Hidden Self*, excerpted from *The Fireside Treasury of Light*. New York, Simon & Schuster, 1990.

Kushner, Harold. *When All You've Ever Wanted Isn't Enough*. New York: Summit Books, 1986.

Latham, Ronald. trans. *The Travels of Marco Polo*. New York: Abaris Books Inc., 1982.

Laury, Jean Ray. *The Creative Woman's Getting-It-All-Together At Home Handbook*. New York: Van Nostrand Reinhold Co. Pub., 1977.

Lowry, Lois. *Anastasia Krupnik*. New York. Bantam Books Inc., 1983.

McLaughlin, Jack. *Jefferson and Monticello: The Biography of a Builder*. New York: Henry Holt and Co., 1988.

Michaud, Ellen, and Alice Feinstein. *Fighting Disease*, Emmaus, Pennsylvania: Rodale Press, 1989.

Nadel, Laurie. *Sixth Sense: The Whole Brain Book of Intuition*. New York: Prentice Hall, 1990.

Nicrenberg, Gerald. *How To Give Yourself Good Advice*. New York: Nierenberg and Zeif, 1986.

Nin, Anaïs. *The Early Diary of Anaïs Nin 1914-1920*. New York: Harcourt Brace Jovanovich, 1978.

Oldham, John M., and Lois B. Morris. *The Personality Self-Portrait*. New York: Bantam, 1990.

Ormrod, Jeanne Ellis. *Using Your Head—An Owner's Manual*. Englewood, NJ: Educational Technical Pub., 1989.

Pennebaker, James W. *Opening Up The Healing Power of Confiding in Others*. New York: Avon Books, 1990.

Rainer, Tristine. *The New Diary*. Los Angeles: J.P. Tarcher/ St. Martin's Press, 1978.

Rawson, Hugh, and Margaret Miner, selected by. *The New York International Dictionary of Quotations*. New York: E.P. Dutton, 1986.

Ray, Michael, and Rochelle Myers. *Creativity in Business*, New York: Doubleday, 1986.

Reader's Digest Association. *Getting the Most Out of Life.*
Pleasantville, NY: 1955.

Resource Contributors, Fantino, Edward, et al. *Understanding Psychology.* Del Mar, California: Ziff-Davis Pub., 1974.

Restak, Richard. *The Brain Has A Mind Of Its Own.* New York: Harmony and Crown Pub. Inc., 1991.

Rico, Gabriele. *Writing The Natural Way.* Los Angeles: J.P. Tarcher, 1983.

—. *Pain & Possibilities.* Los Angeles: J.P. Tarcher, 1991.

Robbins, Anthony. *Awaken the Giant Within.* New York: Summit Books, 1991.

Servan-Schreiber, Jean-Louis. *The Art of Time.* Reading, MA: Addison-Wesley Pub., 1988.

Silverstein, Shel. *A Light in the Attic.* New York: Harper & Row Publishers, 1981.

Simon, Sidney B. *Getting Unstuck.* New York: Warner Books, 1988.

Stock, Gregory. *The Book of Questions.* New York: Workman Pub., 1987.

Strong, George Templeton. *The Diary of George Templeton Strong.* Nevins, Allan, and Milton Halsey Thomas, ed. Seattle and London: University of Washington Press, 1952.

Tatelbaum, Judy. *You Don't Have To Suffer—A Handbook.* New York: Harper & Row, 1989.

Thakkur, G. Chandrashekhar. *Introduction to Ayurveda The Science of Life.* New York: Asi Publishers Inc., 1974.

Thurman, Chris. *The Lies We Believe.* Nashville: Thomas Nelson, 1989.

Utian, Wulf H., and Ruth S. Jacobowitz. *Managing Your Menopause.* New York: Prentice Hall, 1990.

Viorst, Judith. *Necessary Losses.* New York: Simon & Schuster, 1986.

Waitley, Denis. *Being The Best.* Nashville: Thomas Nelson Publ., 1987.

—. *Seeds of Greatness.* New York: Pocket Books, 1983.

—. *The Psychology of Winning*. New York: Berkley Books, 1987.

Wholey, Dennis. *When The Worst That Can Happen Already Has*. New York: Hyperion, 1992.

Winokur, Jon. *True Confessions*. New York: Dutton/Penguin Books, 1992.

Witkin, Georgia. *Quick Fixes & Small Comforts*. New York: Villard Books, 1988.

Bibliography: Articles

Atkins, Andrea. "Mental Health Checkup." *Better Homes and Gardens,* July 1992, 41-42.

Blodgett, Harriet. "Dear Diary: How Do I Need You? Let Me Count the Ways." *Los Angeles Times Sunday Magazine.*

Campbell, Andrea. "Rhythm and Snooze." *The Village Voice,* July 1992, 12.

—. "The Relapse with Telling." *The Village Voice,* July 1992, 14.

Case, Joyce. "She Reaches For Her Pen, Not Her Plate." *Prevention,* October 1989, 130-132.

Diamond, David. "Bound To Worry?" *Health,* July/August 1992, 94-96.

Dolnick, Edward. "Snap Out of It." *Health,* February/March 1992, 86-90.

Elias, Marilyn. "Suppressing Emotions May Shorten Your Life." *USA Today,* Aug. 20, 1991, 6D.

Epstein, Robert. "The Lost Art of Letter Writing." excerpted from *East West,* June 1987: *Utne Reader* May/June 1989, 92.

Fensterheim, Herbert, and Jean Baer. "Why Me?" *Health,* June 1988, 45-46.

Friedman, Lisa. "The Pleasure Principle." *New Woman,* December 1992, 73-74.

Garland, Marcia. "I Battled Low Self-Esteem." *Signs of the Times,* May 1991.

Gibble, Kenneth. "The Family Genesis of Greatness." *Signs of the Times,* May 1991.

Hathaway, Nancy. "Dancing With Your Dark Side." *New Woman,* December 1992, 64, 66-67.

Johnson, Catherine. "How Much Can You Change?" *New Woman*, March 1992, 46-50.

Jordan, Nick. "Self-Management: When to Lie to Yourself." *Psychology Today*, June 1989, 24.

Levoy, Gregg, "Power Lounging." *Writer's Digest*, February 1993, 76 & 80.

McGee, Kelly Good. "Careerwise: Job Burnout—Symptoms and Solutions." *New Woman*, March 1992, 128.

McMahon, Ed. "What To Do When It's Time For A Change." *Parade Magazine*, May 17, 1992, 18-19.

Moore, Judith. "Save Your Life: Notes on the Value of Keeping a Diary." From the Baltimore City Paper. *Utne Reader*, May/June 1989, 90-93.

Pennebaker, J.W., M. Colder, and L.K. Sharp. "Accelerating the Coping Process." *Journal of Personality and Social Psychology*, American Psychology Association, Inc. vol. 58, no. 3, 528-537, 1990.

Schecter, Bruce. "Why Time Flies." *McCall's*, October 1991, 114-115.

Scheele, Adele. "How Ambitious Are You?" *Working Woman*, March 1992, 30.

Sox, Aileen Andres. "The Spanking I Had Never Forgiven." *Signs of the Times*, May 1991.

Stark, E. "Take 2 Self-Help Books and Call Me in the A.M." *Psychology Today*, June 1989, 23.

Sykes, Charles. "The Ideology of Sensitivity." Reprinted by permission of IMPRIMIS, the monthly journal of Hillsdale College." vol. 21, no. 7 July 1992.

Taitz, Sonia. "The Secrets A Woman Should Never Tell." *McCall's*, July 1992. 82-89.

Thomas, Ellen Lamar. "Learning From Your Lumps: How Do You Handle Criticism?" *Signs of the Times*, May 1991.

Bibliography: Other References

Christophers, The (pamphlet). "Dealing with Anger." *News Notes*, 12 E. 48th St., New York: June 1989.

Pennebaker, J.W., E.D. Buhrfeind, S.P. Spera, and D.B. Morin. *Expressive Writing and Coping with Job Loss*. Unpublished manuscript, Southern Methodist University, Dallas, 1992.

Notes

Notes

Notes

Notes

Notes

Notes

Notes

Notes

Notes

Notes

Please . . .
judge our books by their covers.

We can't do justice to the Bob Adams, Inc. line of blank books here, but you can by visiting your local bookstore. Once you take a look at the dozens of striking, evocative designs, you'll know you've come upon a different kind of personal journal.

Of course, there's more to these books than the most attractive cover designs on the market. The pages are spacious and attractively laid out, and the paper stock is a cool, easy-on-the-eyes white. And at just $3.95 each, you'll probably want to pick up more than one. But be forewarned that it won't be easy. There are thirty exquisite covers to judge.

The Blank Book Series
designed by Janet Anastasio.
Bob Adams, Inc., Publishers.

Softcover, $5\frac{1}{2}$" x $8\frac{1}{2}$", 160 pages, $3.95

Available in bookstores; if your bookstore is out of stock, you may order by calling 1-800-872-5627 and charging the order to your Visa or Mastercard. (There is a $3.75 charge for shipping.) *Please check your bookstore first.*

Quick . . .
what's the difference between "CALVARY" and "CAVALRY"?

Or "affect" and "effect"? How about "parameter" and "perimeter"?

Lots of people need a quick and authoritative way to identify and define the most troublesome common words. The usual approach—stalling for time until you can grasp the context of what the person has just said—has its limits. If only there were a list, not of every word (after all, reading dictionaries is no one's idea of fun), but of the *right* words, the ones that are used frequently but don't quite register when you come across them.

The Words You Should Know features straightforward, succinct definitions and sentence examples of 1,200 tough-but-common words. It's the kind of book that can get you out of a jam, improve your performance at school, and help advance your career.

And that's no hyperbole, rigmarole, or embellishment.

The Words You Should Know
by David Olsen.
Bob Adams, Inc., Publishers.

Softcover, $5\frac{1}{2}$" x $8\frac{1}{2}$", 272 pages, $6.95.

Available in bookstores; if your bookstore is out of stock, you may order by calling 1-800-872-5627 and charging the order to your Visa or Mastercard. (There is a $3.75 charge for shipping.) *Please check your bookstore first.*

About the Author

Andrea Campbell is an Arkansas-based freelance writer who has published some thirty-one articles for periodicals such as *Careers*, *Career World*, and *Educational Oasis*. She is also the author of *Great Games, Great Parties*. Ms. Campbell has been keeping a personal journal for most of her adult life.